PRAISE FOR BOOKOLOGY

As both a writer and a friend, it brings me so much joy to share my thoughts on *Bookology*—a brilliant blend of storytelling, strategy, and inspiration by Stephanie Larkin.

Stephanie has done something truly special with this book. *Bookology* isn't just about writing a book—it's about understanding how your book can become the bridge between your passion and your purpose. With her signature warmth, wit, and wisdom, Stephanie guides readers through an engaging allegorical journey that is as entertaining as it is enlightening. (Yes, I found myself smiling more than once at the characters and their antics!) As someone who has worked with many aspiring authors, I can say with confidence that this book is a gift for anyone wondering how a book might fit into their life or business. It's practical without being preachy, full of real-world takeaways nestled inside a charming narrative that makes you want to keep turning the pages.

Stephanie's voice shines through—encouraging, empowering, and always supportive. If you've ever dreamed of writing a book but didn't know where to begin, *Bookology* is your gentle nudge (or firm push!) in the right direction.

I'm so proud of Stephanie—not only for this book, but for the way she continues to champion authors and help people find their voices. *Bookology* is a must-read for anyone ready to take that leap and tell their story.

~Lisa Pulitzer, New York Times bestselling author

"Stephanie Larkin aims to unleash people's "inner author" through her Red Penguin publishing house and in her latest work, *Bookology*, she tells you how to do it. Creatively written as a fictionalized case study, *Bookology* is a must-read for anyone who's ever thought about writing a book but got stumped at how to do it. In easy digestible prose, Stephanie makes the case that anyone can write a book and, moreover, why they should, for both personal or professional reasons. A gold mine of information from a seasoned expert in independent publishing."

~Christina Hoag, author of novels *Law of the Jungle, Skin of Tattoos* and *Girl on the Brink*.

"*Bookology,* written by a seasoned professional, is the toolkit every entrepreneur needs in order to successfully transform and grow their business."

~ Carol Hoenig, author and publishing consultant

"A smart business book tucked inside a clever novel!"

~ Grace Sammon, Award winning author and radio host

"Presented as a light fictional story, *Bookology* morphs ultimately into a comprehensive guide to writing and publishing. A unique treatment of an important non-fiction topic, *Bookology* is a must-read for those in all fields who wish to enhance their professions and projects by writing and publishing a book."

~ William John Rostron, author of *Band in the Wind* trilogy

"If a chef, pro or amateur, wants to improve in the kitchen, Julia Child's books *Mastering the Art of French Cooking* are the bibles. She was the master!

If a small business owner wants to put themselves on the road to success and improve their bottom line, the go to source is *Bookology* written by a successful entrepreneur in the writing and publishing industry. Stephanie Larkin is the master in her world!"

~ Michael Vecchione, author of *Fallen Angel* series

Bookology by Stephanie Larkin has to be the first to suggest the combination of starting up a business and writing a book about that business. Who would be crazy enough to consider both? Larkin's book is a game-changer for aspiring entrepreneurs. If you're dissatisfied with the same old marketing approaches to increasing sales, obtaining the client list you always wanted, and being excited about your work, then take a look at *Bookology*. This book could be the most powerful tool in your toolbox. It certainly is a masterclass in increasing your sales while attracting the clients best suited for your business. Larkin has created a step-by-step story packed with actionable advice for crafting a book to increase your sales, including an entire section of templates that inspire action and ensure success."

~ Donna Keel Armer, author of *The Cat Gabbiano Mystery Series; Solo in Salento: A Memoir*; numerous short story anthologies

---

"Stephanie Larkin has masterfully captured what every aspiring author and entrepreneur needs to know: writing a book isn't just about publishing, it's about positioning, purpose, and creating meaningful impact. As someone who has worked directly with Stephanie on my own book *Holistic Impact: The Ubuntu Polder Journey*, I've witnessed her rare gift for truly caring about the author and their message, while helping them unlock their voice and business potential. *Bookology* is an essential resource for anyone ready to turn their expertise into influence."

~ Bruno Olierhoek, Author of *Holistic Impact: The Ubuntu Polder Journey*

"I'm rooting for Sarah.

You had me at "keeping three kids occupied in the bridal suite" and from that moment on, I was all in.

Bookology is smart, savvy, and sneakily motivating. Watching Sarah, burnt-out, overwhelmed, and totally relatable (I WAS Sarah some years ago), transform her business (and life) by writing a niche book is part story, part strategy, and 100% a kick in the pants to finally consider writing your own.

The storytelling? Spot on. The practical how-to? Laid out so clearly that it feels totally doable, even if you've been stuck in "I could never write a book" land. And the clever use of everyday scenes (like networking events and scrappy video tricks) makes the whole thing feel familiar, friendly, and kind of like a chat with a wildly helpful friend over coffee, if you had a friend with book publishing know-how!

I found myself nodding, highlighting, and dare I say it, getting inspired to write another book myself. *Bookology* doesn't just plant the seed. It waters it, shines a light on it, and gives it a full calendar of growth tactics.

Highly recommended for anyone ready to turn their expertise into opportunity and their story into a sales tool."

~ Adrian Miller, Content Alchemist

"*Bookology: Grow Your Business and Boost Your Expertise Through Book Publication"* is a 'must have' for anyone considering writing a book. In this short, easy-to-read story, future writers get instructive tips on everything they need to know, from selecting their target audience to structuring their book and writing query letters to publishers. I enjoyed reading *Bookology* and even learned a few tips from Stephanie that I can pass on to my writing clients!"

~ Pat Kramer, Business & Memoir Book Writer and Editor

"*Bookology* is an inventive hybrid of novel and entrepreneurial how-to. Written in sunny prose, the story of Sarah's journey to write a book to promote her business creates suspense that propels us through the instructions. Through Sarah's book coaching class, the reader walks in the shoes of a variety of entrepreneurs, from kitchen designers to financial planners. There's something here for everyone, including an entrepreneur who realizes she's gotten off on the wrong foot. Sarah's coach cleverly employs the Socratic method of asking the characters questions, and through their answers, we can imagine our way into writing our own business-promoting book, anticipating pitfalls before they occur. Ending with a set of generative questions and an index of book ideas, *Bookology* is quality instruction delivered with exuberance, instilling the knowledge, inspiration, and confidence to launch a venture of our own."

~ Lâle Davidson, author of the NIEA award-winning novel *Against the Grain*

BOOKOLOGY

GROW YOUR BUSINESS AND BOOST YOUR EXPERTISE THROUGH BOOK PUBLICATION

STEPHANIE LARKIN

Bookology

Copyright © 2025 by Stephanie Larkin

All rights reserved.

Published by Red Penguin Books

Bellerose Village, New York

Library of Congress Control Number: 2025911764

ISBN

Digital 978-1-63777-733-6

Print 978-1-63777-734-3

Audio 978-1-63777-735-0

No part of this book may be reproduced in any form or by any electronic or mechanical means, including information storage and retrieval systems, without written permission from the author, except for the use of brief quotations in a book review.

CONTENTS

PART ONE
BOOKOLOGY

1. Living the Dream??? — 3
2. Write a book? What a Novel Idea! — 8
3. Establishing Your Goals — 15
4. Types of Books — 35
5. Leveraging Technology in Writing Your Book — 68
6. Repurposing Your Writing — 89
7. Meeting your Audience's Expectations — 102
8. Book Description and Pitch — 113
9. Paths to Publication — 126
10. It's Party Time! — 142

PART TWO
TAKE ACTION

1. Why Write a Book — 151
2. How Your Book Will Transform Your Business — 156
3. Establishing Your Goals — 161
4. Eight Types of Books — 169
5. Your Writing Style and Methods — 179
6. Repurposing Your Book Content — 189
7. Judging Your Book by its Cover — 196
8. Crafting a Winning Description — 204
9. Points About Publishing — 210
10. It's Time to Celebrate! — 220

PART THREE
A-Z BOOK IDEAS

Alphabetical List by Profession — 229

Begin YOUR Journey!	267
About the Author	269
Also by Stephanie Larkin	271

PART ONE
BOOKOLOGY

The Book That Changed Everything

Sarah's wedding planning business looked flawless on the surface—beautiful photos, glowing reviews, and an overflowing calendar. But behind the scenes, she was drowning. Burned out, uninspired, and constantly saying yes to the wrong clients, Sarah was stuck in a cycle of busyness with no real growth. That is, until she discovered a surprising secret: publishing a book could be the ultimate key to standing out, scaling up, and finally working with clients who truly valued her expertise.

Part 1 of *Bookology* is a compelling business allegory that follows Sarah's journey from exhaustion to empowerment—showing how sharing her story transformed not just her business, but her entire life.

1
LIVING THE DREAM???

"Thank goodness *you* are running this wedding!" Emma exclaimed.

Sarah had been working with Emma, a rather high-maintenance bride, as her wedding planner for the past several months. Desperation showed in Emma's distraught expression. "My cousin brought her three young children—ages 3, 5, and 8—even though I explicitly said 'no children' on the invitations, and now she's pouting at the idea of leaving. Could you possibly set them up in the bridal suite? If you could watch them for a little while, I'll get my aunt next, and we can take turns so they don't disturb the reception."

Sarah suppressed a sigh. She hadn't entered the wedding planning business to become a glorified babysitter, but compared to some of the other challenges she'd faced that day, babysitting seemed like a minor inconvenience.

Already that morning, she'd had to redistribute flowers in the table arrangements because the florist hadn't sent enough for all the tables, opened several bottles of wine because the bar staff was short-handed, and circulated photos of the groom's ex, who was threatening to crash the wedding, to the security staff. And, in what felt like the ultimate indignity, she'd held up the bride's gown while Emma used the restroom.

Sarah had known that being a wedding planner would require handling a multitude of day-of duties, but she'd hoped those tasks would be balanced by opportunities for creativity—fun designs, themed weddings, and implementing unique high-end ideas. She had even envisioned hiring an assistant to handle the less glamorous aspects of the business down the road. Unfortunately, most of her clients had been budget-conscious brides, making the idea of extra help out of the question.

"Sure, Emma," Sarah said with resignation. "Let me run ahead to the bridal suite and make sure there's nothing unsafe for children."

She hurried to the bridal suite, unplugging curling irons and stowing makeup to prevent any potential messes. She had barely finished unplugging the hair appliances when three children burst into the room. Their mother, Emma's cousin, barely paused before turning to leave. "Thanks for taking the kids. See you later!" she called over her shoulder.

Sarah didn't even ask for the woman's name.

"Hi, kids! I'm Sarah, the wedding planner, and you are—"

Before she could finish, the three children were everywhere at once, exploring every corner of the room and finding every item she hadn't childproofed quickly enough. She scrambled to keep up, snatching items out of their hands or moving them to higher shelves as fast as possible.

Five minutes later, the room was finally safe, Sarah felt frazzled, and the children, already bored, wanted to return to the reception.

"No, no," she blurted, "we're going to stay here. We can play some wonderful games together!" She did not know what sort of games would keep the children entertained in a room where she had just hidden anything remotely interesting.

She briefly considered playing a round of "What don't you want to be when you grow up?" and declaring that wedding planner shouldn't be on anyone's list.

Sarah thought back to her own wedding two years earlier, which remained her favorite event ever. She wasn't sure what she had loved more—the day itself, when she and Ryan became husband and wife—or all the planning leading up to it. Of course, the day was special, but she had adored the research, decisions, and creativity involved in organizing the event.

After the wedding, many guests had commented on how beautiful it was, some even suggesting that she should become a wedding planner. When Sarah mentioned the idea to Ryan, he'd been enthusiastic about the idea. Starting her own business seemed like a wonderful way to channel her passion for wedding planning, and thankfully, she would make—not spend—money. He'd encouraged her, confident that she had plenty of ideas she hadn't been able to use for their own wedding.

He hadn't been wrong. Sarah had filled countless notebooks and Pinterest boards with ideas. She had hoped that as a wedding planner, she could bring those dreams to life—on someone else's dime. But her reality had been different. Most of her clients wanted traditional, low-budget weddings. Her grand ideas remained untouched, and she often handled tasks she hadn't expected, like babysitting children.

Now, locked in a bridal suite with three rambunctious kids she didn't even know, Sarah wondered if she should abandon her dream of running her own business. She still felt she had so much to offer as a wedding planner, but there had to be a better way to make it work.

For now, though, she had to survive the next hour.

"Well," she said brightly, "perhaps we can play a little game?" She wracked her brain, trying to think of something that might distract the children from their boredom.

Then, inspiration struck. Pulling out her phone, she asked if they had favorite videos they wanted to watch. Four people squeezing in front of a small iPhone screen wasn't ideal, but it would do until Emma's aunt or cousin arrived to take over. As the children settled down, Sarah leaned back and sighed. There had to be a way to find joy and creativity in her work again—without babysitting on the side.

THINK ABOUT ...

Many times our life—and work—doesn't pan out quite as we expected. Think about a time in your life when the vision of what was to be didn't align with reality. Was there anything you could do in order to rectify the situation? Do you wish you had done anything differently?

Whether one works for a large company or owns their own business, the realities of work don't always align with one's vision. Where in your professional life are you feeling a disconnect between your desires/expectations and the reality of your situation? Does it have to do with the type of people you work with? The actual work you do? Another aspect of work?

Whether it's your commute or your client base, identifying the areas causing you stress—or not bringing you fulfillment—is the first step to making a change. Think about potential areas for change in both your personal and professional life. While you may not tackle them all today, bringing them to the front of your mind and writing them down means you are already halfway there to changing your life.

2
WRITE A BOOK? WHAT A NOVEL IDEA!

"I've been in business for just six months, and I feel stressed out already," Sarah complained to Ryan. A high school history teacher, he had little exposure to the working of corporate America, much less the "ins and outs" of self-employment, but he was as supportive of Sarah as any husband could be. "Starting my own business sounded like such a fabulous idea. I couldn't wait to plan weddings with beautiful décor, fabulous gowns, and everything cinematically integrated—just like our wedding. But instead, I feel like I'm stuck blowing up balloon arches, memorizing pictures of warring ex-spouses to keep them separated, and babysitting unwelcome children who suddenly show up at wedding receptions."

Ryan replied, "Are you thinking you'd rather go back to working for someone else? I thought you liked the idea of striking out on your own."

"Owning my own business and calling the shots is exactly what I want to do," Sarah explained, "but what I'm actually doing day-to-day is so far from what I wanted." She was certainly grateful that her business had grown and that she had wedding clients, but she longed to raise her rates and work with her ideal client base. Still, she was afraid of rocking the boat.

"Ryan, I have to go. I'm going to a networking meeting with some business friends of mine. I'm sure I'll hear from others that they're in the same boat, and misery sure loves company. And you're right, at least I'm not working for someone else. I am absolutely living the dream of being self-employed and running my own business—even if I do have stressful moments."

Sarah drove to the networking event, thinking about her own business. *I'm sure there are others who have it much worse than I do. At least I have clients!* she thought.

At the meeting, Sarah sat next to Michelle, a woman she had met previously and who always seemed so calm, cool, and collected. Meanwhile, Sarah was busy answering text messages from frazzled clients while the meeting was going on.

"Your business certainly is keeping you busy," Michelle observed as she saw Sarah grab her cell phone for the fourth text in as many minutes.

"It does," Sarah said, "and I am so grateful to have customers so early in my new business, but I look forward to the day when I can finish an entire meal without being interrupted. I'm sure that's way, way down the line!"

Michelle smiled. "Is it you need to delegate more work to others? Or perhaps take on fewer customers so you aren't so frazzled?"

"Fewer customers would definitely help my schedule," Sarah admitted, "but it wouldn't help my pocketbook."

"Maybe you need to raise your rates so that you can afford to take on fewer clients," Michelle suggested.

"That sounds amazing," Sarah said. "And along with taking on fewer clients, I'd love it if they were all a little more creatively-minded and interested in high-end weddings. I'm kind of tiring of the more generic weddings I seem to get over and over. How do you do it in your business, Michelle? Do you have fewer clients, and are they more of what you want?"

Michelle replied, "As a matter of fact, I do. I absolutely love what I do, but I'm much more selective about who I take on. This way, I know that everyone I work with is someone who will excite and energize me and my business without it being a drain."

Michelle was a college coach who worked individually with high-achieving high school seniors on selecting appropriate colleges and assisting with their applications and essays.

"Don't you ever feel as if you have to take every single person who comes along?" Sarah asked. "I think I'd be so nervous about turning down business when it appears."

"I felt the same way," Michelle admitted, "but I was able to attract the type of clients I enjoyed working with. Once I was attracting the right clients regularly, I was even able to raise my rates and take on fewer clients so I could give more time to the select few."

"That sounds amazing!" Sarah exclaimed. "How on earth did you get to that point?"

"It all came about because of the book I wrote," Michelle explained. "I worked with a coach named Amy, and it highlighted my expertise in the college application process. It was so beneficial to show this to potential clients. My book's publication established me as an expert. This led me to attract the right kind of clients. It also opened doors to podcasts, workshops, speaking engagements, and other networking opportunities."

"A book!" Sarah exclaimed. "Goodness, I wish I were talented enough to write a book, but that sounds way beyond my reach."

"It certainly doesn't have to be," Michelle continued. "The coach I worked with helped me develop a plan that got me from start to print in just a few months. She also had fabulous ideas for repurposing the information that was going into my book to help expand my social media feeds and to attract even more potential clients through posts and newsletters."

"Wow, that sounds fabulous. It sounds like it really ignited your entire business to publish a book."

"It sure did," Michelle said wistfully, remembering what her business was like before her book. "Before that, I was just as you described—so thrilled any time the phone rang with a potential new client that I took anyone, whether they were really an ideal fit for me or not. Now, I can pick and choose who to work with, and I find I'm running the business of my dreams instead of the business running me ragged."

"That sounds like exactly what I need," Sarah said. "But be honest—was it a complete time and energy drain for you while working on your book? Admittedly, it sounds like having the book is a fabulous idea, but is it going to kill my life while I'm doing it?"

"Haha, not at all," Michelle said. "I found that working on the book actually helped me to develop ideas about my ideal client and focus my own programs, pricing, and mission. Working on the book not only energized my business once it was published, but it truly helped to organize my business during the process. It wasn't awful at all—in fact, I realized I was truly running this business by the seat of my pants before I started my book."

"Do you think a book could work for me? We're in totally different fields!"

"Absolutely! In fact, I know several people in vastly different fields whose businesses benefited tremendously from a book. My brother-in-law is an accountant, and he wrote a book to simplify complex financial concepts for his clients, which also led to more speaking engagements and a larger, more targeted client base. And my old college roommate, Monica, is a fitness trainer, and she published a book about sustainable fitness and wellness, which helped her to attract high-paying clients interested in a more holistic approach to wellness. Writing a book helped them to focus their business AND led to more clients and more money."

"Well, my business could certainly use some direction, as well," Sarah said. "You've known me for a couple of months now from these meetings. Do you honestly think that I could do it, too?"

"Absolutely!" Michelle exclaimed. "I think you'd be a natural. And, I'm thinking of getting engaged soon, and your book about wedding planning would definitely be something I'd want a copy of. Sign me up!"

"Well, I would love to meet this fabulous fairy godmother of a book coach you have," Sarah said.

"It would be my pleasure," Michelle said. "I'll introduce the two of you—as long as I get a first edition copy for myself!"

"You got it!" said Sarah.

THINK ABOUT ...

Surveys say that over 90% of people asked mentioned that they would like to write a book, so it is likely that even before you picked up this book, the thought of becoming an author may have crossed your mind. However, while most people want to write a book, only a tiny percentage actually do. What do you think holds most people back from achieving that bucket-list item? Is it a lack of time? Indecision about what to write about? Or do most quit before they even begin because it seems insurmountable?

A fun fact about Iceland is that over 30% of the adult population has written a book! Iceland truly has the largest ratio of author/citizens of any country—is it those long dark winters that are conducive to writing? Iceland has a long-standing tradition of reading and writing, so people don't see book writing as the unattainable goal that we may see. Do you know others who have written a book? Find some other authors or join a writing group—surrounding yourself with others who have successes will help to build your confidence in writing your own book.

Even if you don't have any authors in your own social circle, follow some online. They'll gladly share insights, and you'll discover they're just ordinary people like you—but people who focused on their goal and wrote a book!

3
ESTABLISHING YOUR GOALS

Sarah returned from the meeting with a much lighter heart than when she had left. The difference was obvious, and Ryan asked, "Wow, were they serving some fun cocktails or something at that meeting of yours? You look like a different person now."

"Well," Sarah said, "I was sitting next to a business owner named Michelle at the meeting, and she was telling me all about how her business became both energized and streamlined from publishing a book. She went from taking every single client that ever called her to getting to pick and choose only those she really wanted to work with. And her credibility as an expert in her field went through the roof! She said it only took a couple of months to get from start to print, and she even wants a copy of my new book about wedding planning as soon as it's ready. What do you think, Ryan? Do you think I can do a book?"

"What a brilliant idea!" Ryan exclaimed. "You know, she's absolutely right. A guy I went to college with just recently released a book, and the first thing I thought when I saw it was that if I ever had a question about that area, I would call him for sure, since he's obviously an expert on it. Without even thinking twice, I put my trust in him, and I would use him in a heartbeat. I think it's a great idea."

"Me, too!" Sarah said. "I've never been so excited. Michelle said she'd introduce me to her book coach—I can hardly wait to get started."

Later, Sarah opened her email to find an introduction from Michelle to her book coach, Amy, and noticed that in Michelle's signature line, there was a picture of her new book, a link for a free sample, and even a video about her book.

Wow, I wish my email signature looked like that! Sarah thought. She immediately shot off an email to Amy, telling her she was so excited about the prospect of writing a book and couldn't wait to meet her.

Sarah was delighted to receive an email back from Amy that afternoon.

"Hi, Sarah," the email read. "So nice to meet you! I love working with prospective authors on their books, and I especially love books that can ignite businesses. Michelle did a fabulous job on her book about the college application process, and I'm so excited that it has helped her attract the clients she most wants to work with and has streamlined her business.

"I love that you're a wedding planner. My wedding was one of the most special days of my life, and I'm sure you love working with brides to bring their visions to life. But I know weddings can also be filled with drama, and that wedding planners sometimes are more like ringleaders than professional designers."

Boy, thought Sarah, *it sounds like she knows me well already!*

"I would love to meet and learn more about your vision for your business and how publishing a book can help you get there. Let's set up a Zoom meeting so we can get started right away. I'd love to meet in person, as well, but if Zoom is easier, then I guess I'll have to wait until I'm handing you a pen to sign autographs at your book launch party to meet you in person."

A book launch party? Sarah thought. *I'm loving the sound of that already!*

Sarah replied quickly, eager to get something on their calendars. Amy was exactly right—she had become more of a ringleader than a designer, and she would certainly like to turn that around. This book project sounded better and better.

At their first Zoom meeting, Sarah had a million questions—and, of course, a million anxieties to go with them. But the way Amy spoke about her other successful clients and even her plans for Sarah's book launch party was thrilling. Her confidence was contagious.

"So let's talk about your business for a moment, instead of books. My goal is to help you create a book that supports and enhances your business goals. To do that, tell me a bit about where your business is right now and what your ideal or dream version of it would look like."

"Oh, I hope you have a cup of coffee," Sarah said. "I have plenty to say on that subject."

Sarah began telling Amy all about her own wedding, which was a dream, and how she really wanted to help other brides fulfill their vision. While she was certainly busy as a wedding planner, she found that rather than becoming a dream maker and working with brides with vision, she was part organizer, part security guard, and part whipping post. Her large workload thrilled her, but it wasn't the kind of work she'd imagined.

"Tell me," said Amy, "what would your ideal client be like? What is the wedding that you would love to plan—that would really excite you?"

"Well, my wedding was very much like a royal wedding, I must admit," Sarah said. "I love royalty! My friends tease me that I know every single fact about the royal families of Europe, and the only movies I watch are those where a girl accidentally marries a prince. I would love to plan weddings for brides who have a vision for making their day not just special for them and their spouse, but also a dream event for all of their guests to attend."

"Wow!" said Amy. "I'm sure there are plenty of brides who would love that kind of wedding but really don't know where to turn. Tell me something: on your website and materials, does it mention anything about royal weddings?"

"I do have a sentence or two about theme weddings—whether you want fantasy, science fiction, Halloween weddings, or royal weddings," Sarah said. "I keep hoping that someone will contact me wanting one of those, but it hasn't happened yet."

"Well, focusing on royal weddings would certainly narrow your field, but the client you would attract would likely be at a higher price point than your current client base. Is that something you're comfortable with?"

"Absolutely," Sarah said. "I would love to do fewer, better weddings than I'm doing right now."

"Here's a thought," said Amy. "How about a book on royal weddings? Perhaps you could write a guide where you talk about the different dresses, flowers, carriages, and tiaras used at each wedding. You could even discuss some of those TV royal weddings, as well. A book like that would position you as a true authority on the subject—making you the first person people think of when they want to plan a royal wedding. Does that sound like a book you'd like to write?"

"Absolutely! It sounds like a book I definitely want to read, as well, but I could probably write that book with my eyes closed. I don't think I even need to look anything up! I bet there aren't too any people who know the fabric of Queen Isabella's wedding gown when she married King Ferdinand—or the significance of the flowers that decorated Queen Elizabeth's reception!"

"Well, then, there we have it!" exclaimed Amy. "The perfect book that will get you the clients and create the business you want. And I must admit," she continued, "that I, too, got up early to watch the royal weddings, and I can't wait to read your book. So let's figure out exactly how your new book can focus your business and attract the right clients. By establishing your goals at the beginning, you can shape your book's content and tone to align perfectly with what you want to achieve."

"That sounds great! And while I know that royal wedding anecdotes will simply pour out of me, I want to be sure that I am writing the right book to bring my business to the next level."

"So let's brainstorm together about your life and your business after you publish your book. Describe to me your ideal client, including their budget, style, and interests."

Sarah thought about her ideal client—a bride with a generous wedding budget, committed to realizing a vision for her wedding, and one who has had a wedding Pinterest board since grade school. This client loves to watch romantic comedies, is a planner at heart, and wants their wedding to be not only beautiful but memorable. The more Sarah thought about working with such weddings, the more excited she became. "Do you really think it could happen—that I could work with high-end weddings for people with exceptional taste and free-flowing cash? Can a book really make my business dreams come true?" Sarah asked nervously.

"That's the goal!" Amy exclaimed. "To attract first—as a reader—exactly the type of client you want for your business. While we are creating an ultimate client profile, that same person will be our target reader, so we'll want to tailor the book to that type of person. For example, if your goal was to attract academic types, we would want to fill your book with pages of text and statistics that would appeal to that type of reader. From what you are describing, I imagine a book filled with beautiful photos, loads of fun royal wedding facts, and resources such as royal music playlists, cake flavors, and flower preferences. Does that sound about right?"

"Absolutely! Something beautiful to look at, but fun to read. Not dry and boring with pages and pages of text, but something snappy and accessible."

"Great thinking! So your first step will be to dive into the person who is your target reader—and client—and think about everything from their favorite colors and movies to their social media preferences, so that we can target the writing—and promotion—of your new book to the right audience. Next, I want you to answer a set of questions that I will email to you. I have a group of future authors that will meet together so that we can share our ideas with others on the same path. You'll be sharing your responses with the other members of our group so that when we have our first Zoom meeting all together, you already know a bit about each other. Look at the questions and please send me your responses by Monday evening."

"Sounds like a plan! I'll get cracking right away, especially while everything is fresh in my mind." Sarah logged off and opened her email to find the questions from Amy:

Name:

Whew, thought Sarah, *an easy one!*

```
Sarah
```

Describe your current business. Be sure to mention the types of people you work with, as well as the work/service that takes up the largest percentage of your time:

```
I am a wedding planner who works with
brides and grooms to create their
special day. Much of my workday involves
vendor coordination, client meetings,
and child wrangling at wedding
receptions.
```

Sarah wondered if she was being too honest, but decided that transparency was the name of the game.

Describe what your business would ideally be like. Who is your ideal client? What would you like to be spending the majority of your time doing?

I definitely know the answer to this one! Sarah chuckled to herself.

> I would love to work with brides with a vision to make their wedding rival a royal wedding. My passion is creating a high-end experience for the couple and guests, so my ideal client would be those with discerning taste and a budget to match. Ideally, I would spend my time curating a unique and elegant experience —not chasing children!

Why/how do you think that writing a book will help your business?

I'm glad I already met with Amy, Sarah thought, *or I'd be unsure how to answer this question.*

> I hope that writing a book on royal weddings will help to attract like-minded clients who have a specific theme and desire in mind for their wedding.

Sarah was glad to finish up her questions while things were still fresh in her mind, and she sent off her answers to Amy.

A few days later, an email arrived from Amy with the responses from the other participants in her group. Sarah was eager to dive in and meet them, as she had been worried that the others would be much further along than she was on this whole book publishing journey. She was delighted to see that this was not the case. Plus, she loved meeting new people, and had been curious about what types of people would also be in a book writing workshop along with her. She clicked on the first set of responses and was pleased to meet a fairly new real estate agent.

Name:

> Kami

Describe your current business. Be sure to mention the types of people you work with, as well as the work/service that takes up the largest percentage of your time:

> I am a real estate agent, fairly new to the field. I loved the idea of becoming an agent and helping people achieve their dreams of homeownership, but honestly, because I lack clients, I spend most of my time posting on social media, waiting in the office for walk-ins, and showing apartments to potential renters for my agency.

Describe what your business would ideally be like. Who is your ideal client? What would you like to be spending the majority of your time doing?

> I would love to be working with actual people—learning about their needs in buying or selling a house, helping them with the specifics like staging their house or visiting new potential places to live, and attending closings—I've never even been to one yet.

Why/how do you think that writing a book will help your business?

> Great question! I have a friend who was new in her field as a home decorator who wrote a book, and it really helped her to get loads of new clients, so I am hoping for the same for me.

Sarah's thrill stemmed from Kami sounding like a beginner, just like her! She clicked on the next one.

Name:

> Mark

Describe your current business. Be sure to mention the types of people you work with, as well as the work/service that takes up the largest percentage of your time:

> In my profession as a financial planner, I help individuals with their financial

matters. I am qualified to assist people with investments and whole life insurance in order to secure their future. I spend most of my time cold-calling potential clients and following up on referrals from current clients.

Describe what your business would ideally be like. Who is your ideal client? What would you like to be spending the majority of your time doing?

I would like to find a way to attract clients to avoid constantly chasing new leads. Meeting even more people with financial planning needs is my ultimate objective. My ideal client would be someone who wants to work with me because they value financial security and who comes to me without me chasing them. I would like to spend my time working with people, rather than finding new people.

Why/how do you think that writing a book will help your business?

To be honest, I'm not really sure. But I've tried other methods—including running paid ads, signing up for LinkedIn Premium, and joining a BNI Networking Group, but while each of these has brought me a client or two, none have been consistent, so I figured I would give book publication a shot.

I may just fit in with this group after all, thought Sarah. *Let's see who's next.*

Name:

Sharon

Describe your current business. Be sure to mention the types of people you work with, as well as the work/service that takes up the largest percentage of your time:

I am a chemistry professor. I love my job at the university, but I can't achieve tenure unless I write a book. Chemistry and teaching take up most of my time, which is perfectly fine with me.

Describe what your business would ideally be like. Who is your ideal client? What would you like to be spending the majority of your time doing?

I'm satisfied with every aspect of my work. Both my colleagues and the students I work with are important to me. I hope to remain there permanently.

ESTABLISHING YOUR GOALS

Why/how do you think that writing a book will help your business?

> I'm here to learn to write and publish a book because academic circles demand it—"publish or perish," as the saying goes. While pursuing my PhD, I wrote a book—my dissertation—but the process was tedious, leaving me with a finished product I didn't even want to read. I hope to write a book that I, and maybe others, will actually enjoy.

Wow, thought Sarah, *I never expected that there would be a college professor in our group. Very cool! Let's see what's next.*

Name:

> Aidan

Describe your current business. Be sure to mention the types of people you work with, as well as the work/service that takes up the largest percentage of your time:

> I own a general contracting company. We do kitchens, bathrooms, and other home repairs. Admittedly, I spend much of my time on low-end projects and one-shot deals, like a leaky roof or cracked

> tile. I spend a lot of time in Home
> Depot buying supplies—not fun!

Describe what your business would ideally be like. Who is your ideal client? What would you like to be spending the majority of your time doing?

> I would love to have smarter, more loyal customers. People may call me for a quick fix but then call someone different for extensive projects—like renovating an entire kitchen or even a house. I wish I got more calls for those long-term, lucrative projects. I'd even hire someone else for the smaller jobs!

Why/how do you think that writing a book will help your business?

> No clue. But my brother-in-law wrote a book. It seems to help his landscaping business, and he keeps rubbing it in my face.

Ha ha—I feel like I already know Aidan—and his braggy brother-in-law!

Name:

> Tina

Describe your current business. Be sure to mention the types of people you work with, as well as the work/service that takes up the largest percentage of your time:

> As a marriage counselor, I help couples navigate their relationships. I work with couples who are on the brink of divorce. I spend much of my time mediating arguments and trying to guide couples toward reconciliation, often unsuccessfully.

Describe what your business would ideally be like. Who is your ideal client? What would you like to be spending the majority of your time doing?

> I would love to work with couples who actually want to try staying together. Too often, counseling is sought as a last resort—when one partner is already emotionally disengaged. In many cases, one person is committed to saving the relationship, while the other has quietly decided to move on. My goal is to support couples who are genuinely willing to put in the effort to make their relationship work.

Why/how do you think that writing a book will help your business?

> I heard a fellow counselor at a national convention, and they were speaking about their book and workshops they were leading with couples in their area in order to improve their marriages. It sounded like the kind of workshops I would love to run myself, and so I thought—like that speaker—I should start by writing a book.

That sounds like a great reason to write a book, Sarah mused, *and who knows, we may end up with some of the same couples as clients, but only five years apart! Two more to go!*

Name:

> Sam

Describe your current business. Be sure to mention the types of people you work with, as well as the work/service that takes up the largest percentage of your time:

> I am a junior political science student in college. I spend most of my time reading, studying, and writing papers for class.

Describe what your business would ideally be like. Who is your ideal client? What would you like to be spending the majority of your time doing?

> I would love to be accepted into a top university to get my master's degree in Environmental Politics. My dream school—the London School of Economics—takes very few applicants, and after looking at the credentials of their current students, I am more than a little discouraged about being accepted. I would love to spend my future—post-graduate—time working with the UN or another international organization on global environmental policy.

Why/how do you think that writing a book will help your business?

> I looked over the current student profiles at LSE and saw a vast range of accomplishments, which really intimidated me! I saw a number of students who had published works, and while there are many things about my application that I cannot change or enhance, I figured that writing a book was something I could actually do. Heck, I write hundreds of pages of papers each semester, so how hard could it be?

Wow, I kind of wish I had thought of that when I was in college! One more to go.

Name:

> Alex

Describe your current business. Be sure to mention the types of people you work with, as well as the work/service that takes up the largest percentage of your time:

> I am a creative arts lover trying to start a non-profit that will bring theater and the arts to students from schools that are lacking arts programs. The school I teach in has no theater program, but I have a love for the theater and majored in it in college. I'd love to do something to expose other students to the arts I love. I now spend most of my time researching potential grants to get started and learning how to run a non-profit.

Describe what your business would ideally be like. Who is your ideal client? What would you like to be spending the majority of your time doing?

> I'm still working out the details, but I

> would love to have after-school programs for creative kids who like theater, art, and dance. And I'd love to be spending my time working with the students instead of writing loads of grants and going to meetings. Is that even a possibility???

Why/how do you think that writing a book will help your business?

> I wish I knew! Admittedly, I'm here because ChatGPT recommended writing a book on a list of "How to jumpstart your non-profit" ideas. I'm not really sure yet what I will write about, but I figured it was worth a try!

Wow, seven people in my group, each with a very different reason for being in this group. And none of them really sounds like an expert. Sarah was relieved and looking forward to next week's group meeting so that she could put a face with all the names. *This is actually going to be fun!*

THINK ABOUT …

Is writing a book sounding a little less intimidating as you learn about Sarah's group of future authors? If you were in this group, how would you have answered these questions?

Do any of Sarah's classmates remind you of someone you know? Do any of them remind you of yourself? What qualities are you seeing that are similar? Which are different?

Do you think that having a group of like-minded people would be helpful in achieving your goals? Or would you prefer to work totally alone? What do you see as the benefits of each?

4
TYPES OF BOOKS

Next, Amy set up a group Zoom meeting with the other future authors that Sarah had only met through their email responses. Amy mentioned that this meeting would focus on the different types of books they could write, and Sarah was excited to meet other authors-in-progress and bounce some of her own ideas off others. After greeting the others and introducing herself, along with a brief slideshow featuring some of her successful authors, Amy dove right into business.

"Welcome, everyone. I am so excited for all of you to meet fellow authors and share ideas. Before we introduce ourselves, I want to first share with you different ways one can structure a book, so that you might consider some of these tried-and-true options. If you browse the nonfiction books in a bookstore or library, you'll see many structural similarities. Instead of creating a new structure for your book, consider using successful past frameworks.

"I sent along to each of you descriptions of the most popular frameworks used in non-fiction business books, but today I'm going to talk about how each of those book 'types' could apply to a particular industry. Then we're going to brainstorm together about the types of books that may be most advantageous for each of our own industries and book goals.

"For illustration, I am going to use a hypothetical future author in an industry that no one on our call is currently involved with—a chef. Let's imagine that we have a chef in our class who would like to write a book in order to increase business. Of course, our first thought should be exactly what goals does our chef have? Tell me, what are some goals a chef might have in writing a book?"

"Perhaps they want to get more catering clients, as if they were going to be catering private parties and such," Sarah replied.

"Excellent thought. And a book could definitely be a window into many more opportunities. What is another goal a chef might have?"

"Perhaps they're trying to make a big splash to get invited to be a head chef at a famous restaurant," Alex added.

"Very good! I can certainly see how a book would help them capitalize on that kind of opportunity. Are there any other goals our chef might have?"

"Is it possible that our chef simply wants to share recipes they love with the world with no ulterior motive?" Sharon asked.

"Certainly that is possible, and sharing information is something that I venture we all would like to do with our books to help people. But since we're all promoting a business, as well, it would make sense to be sure that our book was an opportunity for personal and creative fulfillment, for the sharing of information, and also for building our business."

"What if our chef wanted to get into The Culinary Institute as a teacher?" Sam asked.

"That's a great goal for our chef, and certainly one that a book would most definitely help. I have a few other thoughts for goals and books for our chef, but let's start with the ones you've outlined and look at our list of possibilities. I've given you each a list of the eight most common frameworks—or templates, you might say—for writing a book. They are:

Book Type #1—Book of Ideas/Tips
Book Type #2—Book of Questions
Book Type #3—Case Studies/Stories
Book Type #4—Compilations/Collaborative Books
Book Type #5—How-To Book
Book Type #6—Business Allegory
Book Type #7—Transformational Memoir
Book Type #8—Children's Book

"So beginning with Book Type #1—the book of ideas or tips—that could be anything from 101 ways to use jarred garlic to converting recipes to gluten-free/nut-free. What goals coincide the best for this type of book?"

"Certainly general exposure in a particular specialty area, which could lead to more personal clients," Tina mentioned.

"Absolutely! Many authors find it easier to structure their book as a collection of tips or an A-to-Z guide on a specific topic. For example, our chef could write *101 Cooking Hacks for Busy Home Cooks* or *The A-to-Z Guide to Mastering Flavor*. These formats are straightforward and make the writing process less overwhelming.

What about Book Type #2—the book of questions? Would our chef be able to use that format for any specific book goals?"

"I think that if our chef were looking to gain more clients—either as a personal chef or as a caterer—a book of questions could really work," Sharon answered.

"I agree! For personal clients, questions about nutritional goals, daily schedules, overall preferences and food allergies might be a great reference for a person stocking a pantry and planning for family meals. Or instead, the questions could have to do with event planning—whether they are specific, like wedding meal planning, or more general, like any catered event for 10-1,000 people. How about Book Type #3—the book of case studies or stories?"

"Well," Aidan replied snarkily, "that could persuade others to never enter the kitchen again—depending upon the stories."

"Exactly!" Amy said with a laugh. "Readers love authentic stories that inspire and teach. And if you want to add a collaborative element, you could include stories from other chefs—or even from home cooks—about their culinary mishaps and lessons learned. A mix of entertaining anecdotes and practical lessons could make for an engaging and memorable book."

"Like a collection of kitchen disasters and how to avoid them?" Sam asked, eyes lighting up.

"Yes, exactly!" Amy laughed. "It's relatable, entertaining, and educational. Plus, a book like that naturally positions you as the expert people need to follow to avoid such disasters.

"Book Type #4—the collaborative book brings together multiple voices around a central theme. For instance, since our author is in the culinary industry, they could invite other chefs, nutritionists, food photographers, farmers, or restaurant owners to contribute chapters. Each expert could share their perspective, tips, and advice, giving readers a well-rounded guide to different aspects of cooking, food sourcing, and presentation."

"That sounds like a fun idea and a great way for people to connect with even more professionals in their industry," Kami said, smiling at the thought.

"Exactly!" Amy said. "Collaborative books are fantastic for opening up networking opportunities for the author. Plus, all the contributors benefit—they get visibility, credibility, and the prestige of being featured in a book. It establishes them as experts in their fields while creating a valuable resource for readers. And because the author's role would focus on coordinating the project rather than writing every chapter, it's much less work for them."

"A book that you don't have to write yourself—I certainly like the sound of that!" They all laughingly agreed.

"Book Type #5 is the classic option, a 'how-to' guide, where you provide practical steps and insights on a particular process—in this case, cooking and meal preparation. Imagine creating a comprehensive guide that walks readers through every detail, from selecting the best ingredients and mastering essential techniques to creating delicious meals effortlessly. A book like that could become a trusted resource for home cooks and aspiring chefs alike."

Sam piped in: "I would think that a book like that—focusing on something rather niche and advanced—might be just the ticket for a chef with higher aspirations, like the Culinary Institute or a fancy restaurant."

"That makes perfect sense," Amy agreed. "Book Type #6—the business allegory—is geared more toward general readers in that they learn lessons while reading a story. For example, our chef—if they have a flair for fiction—might consider a mystery book where ingredients keep disappearing from their cupboard, so they need to learn to make substitutions."

"That sounds fun—or perhaps a romance where a character is being wooed by a chef, who teaches her how to cook on their dates," added Sarah, ever the romantic.

"There are so many options for the writer with an active imagination. Book Type #7 is the transformational memoir—essentially the writer's own story as an inspiration to others. Memoirs are a popular choice for readers and writers alike. A memoir works best when it's transformational—where you share a personal story that led you on a journey toward change or enlightenment. For example, our chef could write about their journey into the food industry and the challenges and lessons that came with it."

Tina nodded, already imagining the possibilities. "These are all brilliant!" she said. "If one had the time and energy, they might want to write several books!"

"Honestly," Amy admitted, "most authors I work with are already thinking about their second book before the first one is published. Writing books is like eating potato chips—it's hard to stop at just one!"

Tina grinned. "I can see that. But for now, completing just one would thrill me."

"Book Type #8 is the children's book. Depending upon a person's target market, writing a children's book relevant to their industry might be a great idea. What type of children's book might our chef write?"

"I suppose a cookbook geared for children—is that what you mean?" Alex asked.

"It could be, or it could be something like a story about a chef who added salt instead of sugar to a recipe, and the chaos that ensued. There are plenty of food-related children's books, and if our chef were trying to break into a younger market, a children's book might be just the ticket.

"So now that we all have the different book types and potential applications in mind, I'd like for you each to introduce yourself, your industry, and your book goals, so that we can brainstorm together on book types that would be best for you to consider. I know you got to meet on paper, but now you get to put a name with a face."

"I'll start. My name is Mark, and I'm a financial planner. I'm excited to be here with everyone, but I've been at a loss about how to get started. I figured I would write a how-to book since that's kind of what I pictured all books written by financial planners would be like. Perhaps that's my only framework of reference."

"Thanks, Mark," Amy said. "Can you tell us a bit about what kind of financial planning you do and, perhaps more importantly, what kind you would like to be doing?"

"Well, honestly, I'll take any client I can get, haha," Mark admitted, "although, I know you mentioned when we met that, for business purposes, it would be best to narrow down what I want. It certainly seems a little counterintuitive to narrow the field in order to get more clients, but I get what you're saying."

"Yes, it does seem a little counterintuitive to specialize in order to build your business, but it actually really works. When people see you as a generalist, they figure you're not really great at whatever it is they're looking for. For example, you may go to a general doctor if you are feeling sick, but a specialist to really solve the particular issue. Plus, specialists get paid a lot more money! Mark, is there any particular area you feel an affinity for—one that might be a good focus for specialization?"

"Well, honestly," Mark said, "My recent divorce devastated my finances. That's one reason I went into this field. I think I'd like to help others in similar circumstances."

Tina piped up. "As a marriage counselor, I can certainly see that! Couples breaking up is an incredibly lucrative area. While professionally I prefer to work to keep them together, others come to me looking for help to navigate a non-contentious breakup."

"You're so right," Mark said. "And I'd like to help them work on a non-contentious financial plan. However, I don't see myself working with both parties. I'd rather work with just one side— helping them to protect their assets for themselves and their children."

"Mark, how would you feel about writing a book that speaks specifically to that issue—protecting yourself financially after a divorce? Or, if you wanted a more hopeful spin, you could write about protecting your assets and children in a blended family after remarriage."

"I really like the sound of that!" Mark said. "And I think you're right. Specializing in helping the newly divorced or remarried to protect their assets wouldn't limit my potential clients. In fact, people would see me as exactly what they need because they're in that situation. I suppose I could write a how-to book on protecting assets in a blended family and securing their children's financial future."

"That sounds terrific!" Amy said. "But let's brainstorm a little. Let's think of all eight book types and see what other ideas we can come up with for Mark."

Tina commented, "A collaborative book might be a good idea for Mark. He could bring in someone like me, a marriage counselor, along with a financial planner, a lawyer, an estate planner, and even a real estate specialist to cover different aspects of navigating divorce. Each person could contribute a section."

"I like that idea a lot," Mark said. "And, honestly, it would mean I'd only have to write a portion of the book instead of the whole thing."

Amy added, "Another way to do a collaborative book—if you're set on writing a how-to book yourself—is to include a guest expert for a chapter as a bonus. For example, an estate lawyer could write a chapter on wills and setting up an estate plan for children in a second marriage. That way, you wouldn't have to speak on a subject you aren't qualified for, and it would create a great referral partnership between you and the estate lawyer. The collaboration could be a full book with multiple authors, or just one section with a guest contributor. Having another expert involved also means they'll be excited to share the book, which could expand your audience and business opportunities."

"I like the sound of that," Mark said. "Building referral partners is definitely a major plan for growing my business."

Alex chimed in. "I could picture your book being a series of case studies or real-life stories—worst-case scenarios in divorce. That would definitely scare people into calling you to handle their finances the right way."

"I certainly have plenty of horror stories, that's for sure!" Mark exclaimed. "Unfortunately, they're all too common in my industry."

Amy jumped in. "Mark, if a how-to book is already forming in your mind, you might start each chapter with a short case study—something illustrating the financial pitfalls you're helping people avoid. Just as collaborative books vary in form, many different structures are possible for a case study book. It could be an entire collection of real-life financial horror stories, or you could use a short one- or two-page story at the beginning of each chapter to illustrate the chapter's key lesson."

"I can definitely envision starting each chapter with a story," Mark said. "It sets the scene well and helps people understand what they need to avoid. I can already picture what stories would pair with different chapters."

"Are there any other book types we should consider for Mark?" Amy asked.

Sam thought for a moment. "Mark, you mentioned your personal story—how you became a financial planner after your own financial disaster following your divorce. That sounds like a transformational memoir. Sharing how your experience led you to this career could resonate with readers."

"It's true," Mark admitted. "I became a financial planner because my own finances were a fiasco after my divorce."

Amy nodded. "If you don't think your personal story could fill an entire book, it would make an excellent prologue or preface. Readers love knowing that the author is a real person. If you're comfortable sharing your journey, it could be a powerful way to open your book. A transformational memoir doesn't have to be the entire book—it can be just a few pages."

"I'm loving all of these ideas!" Mark said. "This conversation is making me feel like jumping off this call to start writing right away."

"If Mark deals with people whose finances are devastated after a divorce, I suppose a children's book about kids with no toys after their parents break up would fit the bill—is that what you had in mind?" Aidan asked sarcastically.

"Well, perhaps a children's book wouldn't be a good fit. But if Mark's book develops the way we're discussing, he'll actually be using Book Types 3, 4, 5, and 7 all in one book," Amy pointed out. "I've listed these book types as a guide—sometimes an entire book follows one type, and sometimes you borrow elements from different types. Either way works. The goal is to make writing your book feel like a natural flow instead of a chore.

"Let's move to a different area of expertise. Kami, could you introduce yourself to our group? Then we'll talk about your book possibilities."

"Sure thing! My name is Kami, and I'm a real estate agent. The compilation-style book immediately caught my eye when I first saw the list of different book types. As a real estate agent, I would love to connect with professionals in other industries, especially potential referral partners. I'm picturing my book featuring chapters by real estate attorneys, title closers, home inspectors, moving specialists, and others—covering all aspects of moving and buying a new home."

"That sounds great, Kami! Do you want to focus your business and your book on a specific clientele? For example, do you primarily work with families, older adults, military relocations, or even people with pets?"

"I guess, like Mark, I've just been happy to consider working with anyone who walks through the door and wants to buy a house. Truthfully, my neighborhood clients are primarily older adults who are relocating. Meanwhile, families are the ones moving in."

"Which of those two audiences do you work with more closely—those who are moving out or those who are moving in?"

"I'm actually hired by those who are moving out, but of course, I end up showing and selling their houses to the people moving in."

"In that case," Amy remarked, "I would think you'd want to tailor your book and referral partners toward those who are actually hiring you. Does that make sense?"

"It does! The people who buy the houses are more random, whereas the sellers are the ones who are actually employing me and my various collaborative partners."

"Sounds good," Amy said. "Now, for Kami—do you think any of these other book types might also work? She seems set on the collaborative style, but would any of the other formats make sense for her?"

"Too bad you're aiming for the older people selling their homes, because if you focused on the young families moving in, I could see a children's book all about a family shopping for a home could be cute," Sam said.

Tina chimed in. "I think a book of questions could be very interesting. When someone is selling a house—especially an older person or their family member—they likely have a ton of questions. Consolidating them all into a book would be really helpful."

"That would also help me when meeting with potential clients," Kami said. "Having structured questions to ask would keep me on task."

Amy added, "If you give them a book at your first meeting—something that gives them 'homework' right away—they'd immediately start building a relationship with you. When you give someone a gift, it makes them feel as if there is a relationship already established. They'd feel more connected to you compared to other real estate agents, which could help you secure the listing from the outset. This way, from the moment you walk in the door, you're already one step closer to closing the deal."

"That's a great idea!" Kami said. "I have to admit, closing deals isn't my strongest suit. I often meet with people and then just hope they call me back to sign a listing agreement. Having something that moves that process along would be a tremendous help."

"If that's the case," Amy said, "your book could include a checklist or timeline for selling a house. One of the first items on that list would be to sign a listing agreement with their realtor. When you share the book at your initial meeting, you can point that out on the checklist. Seeing it repeatedly in the book will make them more likely to take action. That way, you don't have to feel awkward bringing it up—it's just part of the process."

"I love anything that helps close a deal," Kami said.

"While we're on the subject of questions, your expert contributors will want guidance on what you're looking for in writing their own chapters—how many pages, what tone, and the intended audience. You could ask each of them to conclude their chapters with a series of questions to help clients work through the process they discuss in their chapters. If you do yours first as an example, it will make it easier for them to follow suit.

"Including such questions would also make the book more valuable to all of your collaborators. Just like you, they could use the book in their client meetings—flipping to the checklist and timeline to guide conversations. The more structured the book, the easier it will be for everyone involved, and it will create a stronger connection between you and your future clients."

Aidan had a thought. "I know a home inspector that could contribute to your book."

"And Kami," Sharon added, "I find moving and buying a house to be one of the most stressful experiences ever. I'm sure you and your contributors have plenty of horror stories that could add excitement to the book!"

"That's a great idea! I'm sure each of my collaborators has something to contribute in that regard," Kami agreed. "Thank you all so much! I came in feeling anxious about writing an entire book on my own, but now it looks like I'll only need to write a short section while guiding others in their sections. That feels so much more doable! I can also see how bringing a copy of this book to client meetings could help keep me and my future clients on track—and close more deals. It'll immediately establish a personal connection, plus they'll appreciate the free gift. And I can picture all my collaborators doing the same thing! This is definitely a win-win all around. Thanks, Amy!"

"Great job everyone! Who's next?" asked Amy.

"Well, I have a very different job than both of you. I'm Sarah, and I'm a wedding planner. Amy and I were discussing my business and all of my frustrations on our call. Very often, instead of actually getting to plan elegant, high-end weddings like I've always dreamed of, I wind up being a babysitter, a go-between, a peacemaker among family members, and even a maid cleaning up after accidents.

"I would really like to attract brides with a vision—those who truly want to make their wedding something special. After speaking with Amy, I realized that my vision leans toward royal weddings. Honestly, I'm obsessed with the Royals! I would have the perfect life if I could plan royal weddings. But instead, I'm hoping to at least attract clients who share that vision—even if they don't have a completely unlimited pocketbook."

Kami chimed in, "I love royal weddings, as well! I woke up early to watch each one of them. And while I don't have an unlimited budget, I'd definitely love to incorporate elements of royal weddings when I get married."

Mark piped in, "You know, we've been talking about books with stories and case studies, often focusing on the horror stories of what happens in business. But what if, instead, you wrote case studies about royal weddings—all the details of every single one? I must admit, I know nothing about royal weddings, but I would guess they don't have too many horror stories."

"That's true, Mark—they have too much money for horror stories!" Sarah laughed. "But I love that idea. Maybe a book called *Royal Weddings of the Past 300 Years* or something similar. I could dive into the details of the dresses, the flowers, the food, and the fancy guest lists. Goodness knows I would love to research and write that book! My only concern is that, listening to all of you talk about your future books, yours have such a direct outreach to potential clients. I would hope a book about royal weddings could actually convert royal lovers into real customers."

"How about including a bonus section?" Amy suggested. "Something like 'The A-to-Z Guide to Planning a Royal Wedding on a Shoestring Budget' or '101 Tips to Make Your Wedding Feel Royal.' That way, the book would be half about historic royal weddings and half about how readers can apply those ideas to their own wedding."

"That sounds great!" Sarah exclaimed. "I love the idea of making it more relatable—bringing it down to a 'regular person' level. While we can't all be Kate Middleton with an unlimited budget, you can find dresses at a lower price point with the same silhouette, or even replicate her bouquet using silk flowers. Little touches like that make a difference."

"I will definitely be one of your first buyers!" Kami exclaimed. "Now, it's true that I don't have a wedding date yet ... or even a boyfriend. But what you're describing is a book I would definitely buy in a heartbeat. And then, I'd want to hire you—

because you've already shown me you're the wedding planner who shares my vision!"

"Thanks, Kami," Sarah said, beaming. "That makes me feel great—my book already has a home. A home on your bookshelf."

Sharon, who had been listening quietly, finally spoke up. "Well, this all sounds like fun and games," she said with a smile, "but I'm a chemist. I need to write a book because I'm at a university, and the rule is publish or perish. If I want to get tenure, keep my job, and work my way up to full professor, I have to publish. But admittedly, I'm not exactly trying to get clients like any of you. The only 'client' I need to impress is the university administration, to show that I'm a published author.

"I need to write something that is reputable and respectable. I wrote my dissertation years ago, but it was dry and boring—certainly not something I could turn into a TED Talk! While I could force myself to churn out another dry, academic book, I'd much rather write something accessible to the world. And maybe … just maybe … I could consider a TED Talk at some point. Wouldn't that be exciting?"

"Well, before we talk about what type of book Sharon might write, let's brainstorm topics in chemistry that might have more universal appeal than just academics."

"I don't know," said Sam. "I failed chemistry in high school."

"Me, too," said Sarah. "Well, I didn't really fail, but I had a tutor because I just didn't get it. And I definitely didn't understand what use I had for chemistry in my life at all."

"That's the thing," said Sharon. "Chemistry absolutely applies to your life! For example, if you like to bake, baking is chemistry. The way baking powder and yeast work, the way different chemicals come together to make bread rise and cakes fluff—that's all chemistry.

"Chemistry is also important in cooking. For instance, if your food is too spicy, you can add a little lemon juice because citrus helps break up the polymers in capsaicin, which makes spicy foods taste milder."

"Really? I had no idea!" said Sam. "I would have paid attention in chemistry class if they had talked about stuff like that!"

"That's so true," said Amy. "I wish they had taught chemistry in a way that applied to real life—just like how I wish they had taught math in a way that related to finances."

"Exactly," added Mark. "Math in school was just a bunch of formulas and fractions that meant nothing to me. It wasn't until I got into finance and learned about things like compound interest I realized how useful math actually is. I wish someone had told me that in 10th grade!"

Sharon thought for a moment. "I wonder if a book about chemical reactions you can use in the kitchen would be appealing to readers. Of course, I also need it to be high-level enough to help me get tenure at the university, but there must be a way to balance the two."

"I'll bet there is!" Amy chimed in. "Just like how Sarah is writing about royal weddings while also including tips on how to make your own wedding feel royal on a budget. I bet you can find a way to make chemistry both accessible and applicable to regular people while also making it academic enough to count toward tenure."

Mark nodded. "How about an A-to-Z guide to chemicals we use every day but have never heard of—and how they work? That could help structure your book."

"I like it," said Sharon. "That definitely sounds workable."

Usually quiet, Sam finally spoke up. "If you're interested in wine or beer-making, that could be a fascinating angle for your book, too. I don't know much about it, but I'd imagine that all alcoholic production is based on chemistry."

"It definitely is," Sharon said. "In fact, many chemistry majors become home winemakers, and some even go into the field professionally."

"That might bring it a little closer to home," Tina said. "Like, why do white wine and red wine taste different? Or what makes whiskey stronger than beer?"

"That could definitely be an interesting book!" Sharon said. "I could even see sales opportunities at breweries—for people interested in the science behind what they're drinking."

"These are all great ideas!" Amy said. "Hey, Sharon—why did you go into chemistry in the first place? Was it because of something like cooking, or …?"

"Actually," Sharon said with a smile, "my fifth-grade science project—one of those giant exploding volcanoes—completely captivated me. I struggled for the longest time to get it to explode. It just wouldn't work—until I finally understood the chemical reaction behind it. After that, I was hooked."

"Well, that might not be enough for a full transformational memoir," Mark said, "but it would make a fantastic introduction to your book. It would help me understand who you are and why you're passionate about chemistry."

"Honestly," he added, "before today's meeting, I assumed all chemists were stuffy, boring people with no personality. Thanks for proving me wrong!"

"Well, I'm a general contractor," Aidan interjected, "and believe me, I have enough horror stories for an entire book."

"I'm sure you do," said Amy, "but you also want to make sure that you're positioning yourself as someone who prevents those things from happening to your customers."

"I get that. I'm almost afraid to tell them about the horror stories," Aidan said. "How can I do both at the same time?"

"Well," Amy asked, "tell me a bit about your process—how people find you and how they decide to hire you for a project."

"I often get a call from someone who either sees an ad or knows someone who has used me in the past. I'll go over to their location and meet with them so I can see firsthand what they want. Then I'll give them a proposal and hope that they accept it."

"And what seems to make or break their decision about hiring you?" asked Amy.

"Most people seem to have already decided before I even walk in the door," admitted Aidan. "If they come from a referral, then that's usually the case, because they've already heard good things—hopefully not horror stories. However, if they come from an ad, I assume they're getting multiple quotes from different contractors."

"And incidentally," Aidan added, "those horror stories usually aren't even about what a contractor does—although, to be fair, there are plenty of bad contractors out there. More often, it's about what's behind the walls of a house that homeowners have no idea about."

Mark chimed in. "I have a thought—what about a book called *101 Things Your Contractor Wishes You Knew*? Maybe 101 is too many—maybe 50 is a better number to start with—but it sounds like there are plenty of things you wish homeowners knew before a project even begins."

"That's for sure," Aidan said. "I also wish they understood the importance of using quality materials. When a homeowner turns down my services because of price, it's not even about my labor costs—it's about the materials I insist on using. I refuse to use anything but the best materials because this is going into someone's home and should stand the test of time. But homeowners don't always appreciate that and, honestly, many of them try to use cheaper materials. I wish they understood how critical structural materials really are."

Kami joined the conversation. "Are you saying that if potential customers were more educated, more of them would choose you?"

"Absolutely!" Aidan said. "An educated customer is my best friend. Once they realize that I'm not spending their money haphazardly—but rather, investing in their home so it appreciates in value—they're much more likely to hire me."

"Well then," Amy said, "that book—*Things Your Contractor Wishes You Knew*—sounds like a great thing to give out at that initial meeting. Handing them that book makes you seem more expert than other contractors, and because you wrote a book, they'll trust you more. And if you leave the book with them, they'll be reading up on all these things—and that could solidify their decision to hire you."

Mark added, "And if, in the course of writing about these things, you want to include some horror stories, that would just make it even more interesting to read!"

"I like it," Aidan said. "Looking down this list of book formats, I see The Book of Questions. I think I'd like to include some questions in mine, too."

Amy asked, "What kind of questions are you thinking about?"

"Well," Aidan said, "there are so many things a homeowner really doesn't know. It would be a good idea to have a section where they can write down important information. For instance, when I enter a home, the owner is often unaware of the material of their foundation, the last update of their electrical system, or the type of heating system they have.

"I think having a few pages with questions like that—so the homeowner can gather and record these details—would be really helpful. And it would make my job much easier if they had all that information in one place."

"That sounds like a great idea," Amy said. "Plus, it would be a valuable resource for homeowners, adding even more value to your book. When you show up to give them a quote, and you also give them a book with that kind of practical information, that's going to make you stand out from other contractors."

"I like it, too," Mark said. "Aidan, I can see this all coming together—the tips, the questions, and the stories. Combining all of those means that writing the book isn't just about cranking out thousands of words—it's more about putting together shorter, useful sections. That sounds much more manageable."

"I can definitely handle that!" Aidan said. "And if not, I could go in a totally different direction and write a children's book—almost like *Bob the Builder*—starring me as the hero!" They all laughed.

"The possibilities are endless," Amy said. "It sounds like you have a solid plan—not just for your book, but for how you're going to approach future customers."

"I'm loving the idea of putting questions in a book—that sounds like it would definitely work for me," Tina piped in. "I'm a marriage counselor, and besides working with couples individually, I'd also like to run group workshops online. Doing so would allow me to work with more people at once, rather than just one-on-one, and it would be a great feeder into my private practice."

"That sounds terrific," said Amy. "A book would be a natural tool to use in your workshops. Do you already have your workshop planned out?"

"I do have much of it outlined," said Tina. "I was picturing a workshop called 'Six Weeks to Reignite Your Marriage,' with different topics each week."

"If you already have an outline," Amy said, "you could literally plug that outline into your book as the table of contents. You could include some of the key concepts people will hear in the workshop, along with the questions you want them to go over for the next week. Your book could be available for sale publicly, or you could use it exclusively for your workshops—whichever you think is better."

"That's a good question," Tina said. "I just presumed it would be public, like I had no choice. But if I do have a choice, I wouldn't necessarily want the entire world to get the same book that workshop participants are getting. It seems like I'd be giving too much away."

"I get that you're concerned about giving things away," remarked Amy. "That's a very common concern among authors—that people won't want to work with them because they already got all the knowledge they needed from the book. But in actuality, the opposite actually occurs. People see the book, get a good idea of what you're all about, and then they want to work with you. They realize that reading the book and taking part in an actual workshop are two very different experiences.

"However," Amy continued, "you could have one public book, and then a separate version with add-ons that you use in your workshop—something that goes above and beyond the regular book. That way, you don't have to worry about workshop participants wanting a discount just because they already bought the public version."

"I like that!" Tina said. "I could really think about what goes into the book and what goes into the add-ons."

Mark chimed in. "That six-week program—I'm curious. Is it meant for marriages that are in trouble or for couples who just want to add an extra spark to their relationship?"

"Great question," said Tina. "And I suppose now that you mention it, I should differentiate between the two. Maybe I'll end up having two workshops: one for couples who want to improve what they already have and one for those who need help to work through specific challenges."

"Well, Tina," Amy said, "before you lay out your workshop and start writing the book, it would be a good idea to figure out which one you want to start with. I imagine people would probably self-select the workshop that best fits their situation based on your book and materials. Does one approach appeal to you more than the other?"

"I suppose, just from a practical standpoint, I'd like to work with couples whose marriages aren't quite in serious trouble yet," Tina said. "Since running online workshops will be new to me, I don't want the added stress of mediating fighting couples while I'm still figuring out the tech side of everything."

"I totally agree with that," Amy said. "I can't even imagine how you, as a marriage counselor, handle fighting couples—never mind in a room full of people on Zoom!"

Sam chimed in, "I'm really impressed with the sound of all these books, but I have a different kind of book and would appreciate your feedback. I'm a college student wanting to get into a prestigious master's program, and a friend's mom suggested publishing a book. Although I love the idea and see the perfect place to add it to my applications, I am stuck on where to begin. I'd like to do that collaborative book and have other people write my book, but I'm afraid that will not fly for the admissions committee."

"Wow—I never thought about publishing a book to help boost your application and get into college, but it does make sense. I may have my 15-year-old start writing now!" quipped Mark.

"I wish I were trying to get into the Culinary Institute—you had fabulous ideas about that earlier," Sam added.

Sharon's ears had perked up. "You and I are in a similar circumstance in that we are both trying to impress academically-minded people—me for tenure and you for admission."

"Yup! And I'd suggest a partnership, but remember, I failed chemistry," Sam laughed.

"What are you studying?" Mark asked, "and where are you applying?"

"I'm studying global politics and want to go to the London School of Economics for my masters. The programs there are very competitive, but I did a semester program there last year and loved it, so it's my #1 choice. And writing a book sounds like a great idea for my application, but actually finding the time along with my schoolwork isn't easy."

"Since you're in school, do you have any papers done or due that perhaps you could use for your book?" asked Sharon. "If you had something already done, perhaps you could expand upon it to make it into a book. Amy, could Sam do that?"

"Absolutely! Just as many people in business combine and repurpose their blog posts into a book, Sam could certainly take work that's already written and work it into a longer manuscript to be a book. In fact, if it was something you already submitted for a grade, Sam, you could even incorporate any suggestions your teacher made on your paper into your new, longer manuscript. Do you have any papers that might fit the bill?"

"I did just do a 20-page paper on the philosophy of politics in developing nations, but I must admit it thoroughly disinterested me. But last semester I did a term paper on the GERD in Ethiopia—that was pretty cool!"

"What is the GERD?" asked Kami.

"The GERD is the Great Ethiopian Renaissance Dam. It's a dam on the Blue Nile, and it's supplying power to much of Ethiopia."

"I hate to sound snarky, but what was so interesting about a dam in Ethiopia?" asked Aidan. "And what is the Blue Nile? Aren't all rivers blue?"

"Great questions—and please feel free to shut me up if I talk way too much about the GERD. My parents are pretty sick of me droning on about it. The country of Ethiopia built the Great Ethiopian Renaissance Dam to generate hydroelectric power, aiming to boost its energy supply, support economic development, and provide electricity to millions of people. Additionally, the dam enhances water storage for agricultural and industrial use, helping Ethiopia achieve greater water security and regional influence. And the Blue Nile is one of the two rivers that flow into the Nile River—the other is called the White Nile."

"And let me guess—the White Nile is white?"

"Not bad," continued Sam, seemingly oblivious to Aidan's sarcasm. "Heavy silt content makes the Blue Nile appear blue, whereas the White Nile's clay content gives it a whitish color. The Blue Nile supplies more of the water to the Egyptian Nile than the White Nile, and the dam is on the Blue Nile. The building of the dam raised concerns in Egypt over potential reductions in its share of Nile water, which is crucial for agriculture, drinking water, and industry. Egypt fears that the dam's reservoir filling and operation could disrupt water flow, especially during droughts, threatening its water security and economy. This led to major tensions in the area, with countries choosing up sides."

"You are obviously passionate about this!"

"I am! It was so interesting learning about how one country's attempt to help their citizens by manipulating natural resources affects others over their borders, and could potentially start a war. But my original paper was 20 pages long—how can I make it into a book?"

"I have a thought—how about adding Book Type #3, the case studies, to stretch your book? Perhaps there are other examples of places where a dam helps one country but hurts another," mused Sharon.

"Or even other environmental issues that have impacts in multiple countries."

"Wow—I can name a half a dozen of those types of international situations right off the bat. Can I really do that—add case studies around the world to pump up my manuscript?"

"Absolutely! What was the title of your paper?"

"It was 'The Great Ethiopian Renaissance Dam and its Effects on The Nile River Basin.'"

"Well, how about your new book being called something like *Power, Politics, and the Planet: The Great Ethiopian Renaissance Dam and Other Fights for Earth's Resources*? That way, your focus would be on the dam—since you already have that section written—but your subsequent chapters could be case studies of other environmental political hotspots around the world."

"You are amazing—you could be a political science professor!" exclaimed Sam. "And I'm thinking that I will have to do a senior year capstone project to graduate—perhaps I could use my new book for that project, as well."

"Wow—a paper that you wrote last year, repurposed as your capstone project, and published to get you into grad school—what a fabulous triple use of one paper!"

"I wish my papers from school could be useful now that I've graduated, but I can't seem to figure out how. I'm Alex, and I'm working on getting a non-profit arts organization off the ground. My school lacks theater and arts classes, and I'm eager to offer them to underserved kids in my community."

"What kind of program will this be, Alex? Will you actually be leading classes in schools or doing something after school or on the weekends?" asked Sharon.

"Honestly, I would love to do both. I've been looking for a space where we can have an after-school program, but I'm hoping that we'll secure grant money to fund different teachers to lead workshops in the schools, so it's more convenient for the students who might not be able to come after school. I've heard that a book can help a non-profit, but I'm really not sure how."

"There are several ways that people have used a book to help to start or promote a non-profit organization. It all depends on what your goals are for the moment because there are different kinds of books that might help at different times. For example, if you're trying to establish why participation in the creative arts is important for young people and you're working toward gaining sponsors and donors for your organization, you might want to write a book about how exposure to the arts helps kids to develop critical analysis and build their self-esteem. That type of book could even include experts such as therapists, teachers, and psychologists."

"Wow, I never thought about that!"

"A book like that could also lead to you to being a speaker—maybe even a TED talk—which would certainly help to give you and your organization credibility and exposure."

"And hopefully, along with credibility and exposure, comes money and support."

"Exactly!"

"You said that there were several types of books I could write. What else did you have in mind?"

"Well, once you get things going, you might want to publish a book of short plays for kids to act out in their classrooms—something easy for the teachers to manage. They could be originals or even public domain works," Amy continued.

"How about if you published a book of plays that the kids in your program actually wrote?" Sam was excited about Alex's project and already wanted to help somehow. "Perhaps that can be your second book, since you would already need to be up and running for that one to come out."

"Wow! I love the idea of featuring the students and getting them published. Can I really do that?"

"Absolutely! I have worked with schools and literary organizations who publish annually so that they can feature the best work of their participants. Such books are terrific for a fundraising activity and also help to show to potential donors all the good work you're doing. Projects like these can become the cornerstone of the calendar each year so that participants have something tangible to strive for. And you can often receive a grant to finance the publication of such a book, which will be more money to put toward your programs."

"Hey, Alex, didn't you mention you were hoping to expand into visual art, as well?" Sam asked. "The art works of your students would make a beautiful book!"

"Amy, are you saying that maybe Alex should write a book about the benefits of creative education for kids first in order to get exposure and build up a donor base to get started, and then publish books featuring the actual program participants to further grow the organization? Wow, a whole non-profit strategy built on books!" Sharon knew that book publication was critical at the university but never thought about how instrumental it could be in other areas.

"Exactly. In fact, while we're all here discussing your first book, I wouldn't be surprised if many of you later find a new book that will further leverage your business. If one book is good, two can be even better. But let's not get ahead of ourselves—today we will focus on Book #1!"

"Sounds good—although I must admit that the thought of publishing each year and featuring our program participants may be something that I want to write into our plans right now, as it will not only give structure to our annual calendar but will also look proactive to prospective donors. I like it!" Alex was feeling more hopeful about the future by the moment.

"So getting back to Alex's first book—one that focuses on the benefits of the arts in education—which book types do you think would be best?"

"I'll admit I have a bias towards the collaborative book. I'm looking at doing one about home buying, and I think it's a great way to include experts and not have to write too much yourself," offered Kami.

"Alex also mentioned not having the arts in school, so perhaps a personal story is in order as well."

"If you could include other stories—or case studies—as well, that would be amazing. I know loads of students who may be good for interviews."

"These all sound terrific—what do you think, Alex?"

"I think I'm ready to get out of this meeting and start writing!" Everyone laughed as they said their goodbyes to get started on their books.

THINK ABOUT ...

Had you ever noticed that books follow the same general format? Fiction books—and even movies—also follow established conventions, and learning what they are and how they can apply to your project is a much better use of your time than reinventing the wheel. Have you ever read a book that followed one of the book types listed? What did you like about the type of book that you read?

There is definitely a range in the different types of books of how much writing and creativity the author will need to do themselves. The least amount would be the collaborative book, and the most creative writing would likely be the business allegory or transformational memoir. What level of involvement speaks the most to you? Why?

Do any of the book types mentioned sound terrible to you—like something you would avoid at all costs? Why do you think that is?

5
LEVERAGING TECHNOLOGY IN WRITING YOUR BOOK

That evening, over dinner, Ryan was eager to hear how the Zoom call went.

"It was amazing!" Sarah said. "It was so nice to meet other business owners who are writing books, and I feel like I'm a minor part of their book development, as well. I can hardly wait to go to all the book launch parties!"

Ryan piped in, "Well, that won't be for quite some time, I'm sure."

"I don't know, Amy laid it out in such a straightforward way that it doesn't seem overwhelming. She spoke about how all the books we read fall into one of eight types—or a combination of them. Now that she said that, I'm looking over some books I have here, and I can actually pick out what type they are. We discussed our businesses and goals, and then, as a group, talked about which of the eight types would be best for each person to write."

"Goodness, is it that clear-cut?" Ryan asked. "Are there really specific types of books meant for each occupation?"

"Well, not quite. It's more like specific types of books that align with your goals for the book and also how much input you want to have. For example, one of the book types was called a 'collection' or a 'collaborative book.' Basically, that means you gather a group of experts in your field and ask them each to write a chapter. That way, you only have to write one chapter —and maybe the introduction, as well."

"Wow," said Ryan. "I can see how that wouldn't take long to do."

"Exactly! In fact, you can even do those through phone interviews. You ask contributors a bunch of questions, then turn the phone interview into text using a transcription tool."

"Interesting, that doesn't sound awful at all. Are all the book types as simple to write?"

"No," Sarah replied. "Some definitely require a lot more input from the author. For example, if someone has an interesting life story or an event that led them to their business, they might be an excellent candidate for writing a transformational memoir. That isn't really me, but there was someone in our group who works with divorced couples—and he's been through a divorce himself."

"I get it—making it personal by telling your own story."

"Exactly. So you could do that for the entire book if your story is interesting enough, or you could just use it for the introduction. For example, in my book, I'm going to talk about our wedding and other weddings I've worked on. That's personal, but I'm not making the entire book about my story."

"So what is your book going to be about?" Ryan asked.

"Well, Amy has been talking with me about my business goals, and honestly, I would love to target high-end brides and weddings. I want brides who have a vision and want me, as their wedding planner, to execute an amazing event—something like brides who dream of having their own royal wedding."

"Well, royalty is certainly in style," Ryan said, as he looked up from the essays on the British monarchy his students had submitted the day before. "How can you capitalize on that?"

"I'm going to write a book that details the royal weddings of the past several hundred years. A book like that would attract people who love royalty and finer things. But I'm also going to include a tip section on how to have your own royal wedding—even if you don't have an entire country at your beck and call."

"That sounds great! I can see how the book targets the right audience while also providing helpful suggestions, which shows that you really know your stuff."

"Exactly! A big part of writing a book is establishing yourself as an expert. I'm hoping that with a book like this, people will see me as the go-to planner for coordinating royal-style weddings—even for commoners! That way, anyone with the right budget and taste for luxury will automatically call me."

"So, what other kinds of people were in your class today?" Ryan asked.

"It was quite an interesting group. There was a chemist who wants to get tenure at the university where she teaches, a general contractor, a financial planner—all sorts of different professions. Each of them had different reasons for wanting to write a book, which meant they would each fall into one of the eight book types—or often a combination of them."

"Do you think everyone is finding it as easy as you?"

"I'm not sure, but I certainly hope so! It certainly seemed that way on the call—everyone was excited to get started because what we were talking about made sense and aligned with their vision. I'm just waiting for an email now because Amy said she'd send each of us a template customized to the type of book we're writing, so we can plug our ideas directly into a framework. I love that idea because, rather then starting from scratch, as Amy says, 'There's no point in reinventing the wheel every single time—start with a framework instead.' My mind is already racing," she continued. "So even while I'm waiting for my framework, I'm going to start researching royal weddings."

Ryan chuckled. "That hardly sounds like work for you! You love that kind of stuff, so looking up all the details probably feels more like a fun project."

"It is a fun project—but a fun project that will also get my book done! I'm so excited—not just to have the book, but about everything I'm going to learn in the process."

After dinner, Sarah got to work at her computer, finding websites and sources for historical details. She decided it would be useful to create a checklist for each royal wedding so she wouldn't forget any details. Her checklist included the names of the bride and groom, their families or countries of origin, their titles, the year of the wedding, the location, and additional details such as the dress, cake, bridal attendants, and other notable aspects. She created multiple copies of the checklist so she could efficiently fill in the details for each wedding she researched—for example, Queen Victoria's—and ensure completeness.

The very next day, an email arrived from Amy with an encouraging letter and a template for Sarah to use in writing her book. Seeing her book take shape thrilled her. If she didn't feel like working on one particular section on any given day, she could switch to another, thanks to the template. Amy also invited her to another meeting—this one about writing tools and overcoming writer's block.

At that moment, Sarah felt unstoppable. But by the third day, she suddenly found it harder to get motivated, and she couldn't figure out why.

Boy, am I glad that meeting about writer's block is coming up soon, Sarah thought. *Sometimes I sit at my computer and the words just fly, but other times—like when I'm writing my tips—I get stuck. I'll be glad to hear Amy's ideas on dealing with that.*

At the next Zoom meeting, Sarah was excited to see the other writers and hear about their progress.

"Before we get started on writing tools and overcoming writer's block," Amy said, "I'd love to hear how everyone is doing this week. Has everyone gotten started on their books—even if it's just a page or two?"

"I sure did!" Sarah piped up. "After our last meeting, I was so inspired—I dove right into researching royal weddings and gathering information."

"I was excited, too," said Aidan. "I started brainstorming all the stories I want to include. I even made a list of people to contact, but I haven't reached out yet. I want to be confident in exactly what I'm asking them to do, so I don't waste their time."

"That's wise," Amy said. "If you're asking people to contribute to your book, you want to be crystal clear in your request so you don't have to go back and make unnecessary revisions. You might even want to ask one person first, see how the conversation goes, and note questions they have. That way, you'll be better prepared to refine your request and maybe even create a checklist for contributors."

"Great idea!" Aidan exclaimed. "I wasn't sure how to manage that, but that makes perfect sense."

The group continued sharing their progress and obstacles.

After hearing from everyone on their progress, Amy dove into the lesson for the day. "I wanted to begin today by talking about two words you may never have heard before: 'plotter' and 'pantser.' Has anyone ever heard those terms before?"

"Well, I suppose a plodder is someone who just plods along. Is that right?" asked Mark.

"Well, that's true for 'PLODDER,'" Amy replied, "but I'm actually talking about 'PLOTTER'—someone who plans out their story in advance."

"So, is that someone who writes the plot?" asked Sharon.

"Pretty darn close," said Amy. "I interview a lot of authors, and fiction writers often describe themselves as either a plotter or a pantser. People who write novels typically fall into one of these two categories.

"A plotter is someone who outlines their book in advance. They decide what each character is going to do and know how the plot will unfold—sometimes down to every single scene.

"On the other hand, a pantser is someone who essentially writes by the seat of their pants. They may have absolutely no idea what's going to happen next. In fact, I've spoken to writers who identify as pantsers, and they've told me stories about sitting at their computers crying because one of their characters had just died. Of course, my reaction is always, 'Well, you were the one who killed them!' But sometimes, pantsers truly don't know what's going to happen next—the story just develops through their fingertips.

"I must admit, I've often been envious of pantsers. The idea of sitting down at a computer and having a story pour out of me —without knowing what's going to come next—is rather amazing. But I suppose the same concept applies to giving a speech. Some people would never dream of standing up in front of an audience without having their entire speech written in advance. Others, however, prefer to just get up and wing it."

"Well, I certainly do that for improv," Alex said, "but can't imagine doing that for a book."

"I get that," said Amy, "and that's why there aren't necessarily just two rigid ways of writing—plotting or pantsing. Even in novel writing, most people fall somewhere in between. Some authors plot everything out in advance, deciding on all the characters and key events, down to which chapters will feature major turning points. But when they sit down to write, they may let the story unfold naturally. If they realize their book is heading in an unexpected direction, they might decide that's a better choice than what they originally planned.

"Likewise, a pantser may start out writing freely but eventually realize they need to create some structure. They might write a few key scenes and then step back to figure out how the story got to that point—essentially plotting in reverse."

"I understand that," said Kami. "If I were giving a speech, I'd like to have some notes—maybe some general thoughts—but I don't know if I'd want to write it all down in advance. I just wouldn't want to forget something important."

"Exactly," said Amy. "I'm bringing this up because understanding this can help you with your own writing. For all of you, this is your first time writing a book, and you don't yet know what process will work best for you. You may have thought that you need to outline everything and make a detailed plan. I sent each of you a template to work from because most first-time authors find that helpful. But when actually filling in the blanks and writing your book, you may find that plotting works—or you may find that it doesn't.

"If you're struggling with a section, maybe take a different approach. Instead of forcing yourself to outline every detail, try dreaming about it. Take a walk on the beach or through the woods. Bring a recorder and just talk about the chapter—perhaps even pretend you are talking to someone or giving a speech about it. Maybe for that part of your book, it would work better to go with the flow and let inspiration guide you. Or, if you work better verbally, discuss the section with someone else. Sometimes, we speak more freely when talking to another person than when sitting alone in front of a blank screen.

"The key is that not every part of your book needs to be written the same way. You can meticulously plan some sections, while letting others develop more instinctively and freely. Give yourself the flexibility to let each part of your book evolve in the way that works best. And if you struggle with writer's block, don't keep trying the same method if it's not working. Try something new.

"Another important thing to remember: you do not need to write your book in order. Many writers don't start at the beginning and work straight through to the end. Even novelists, who are dealing with continuous storylines, often begin in the middle. They might write a pivotal scene first and then go back to add the backstory or fill in earlier events. Some authors even embrace a technique called 'in media res,' which means starting a story in the middle of the action. You've probably seen movies or read books where the first scene is chaotic, and only later do you figure out who the characters are and what's happening.

"My point is, don't feel pressured to write sequentially. And don't feel you need to write each section using the same approach. If you're stuck on a particular chapter—whether it's the introduction or Chapter 6—skip ahead to something you're more excited to write. The best way to beat writer's block is to keep writing, but not necessarily to force yourself through a section that isn't flowing. Come back to it later. Sleep on it. You may find it much easier to tackle the next day. But if you keep banging your head against the wall, you'll just get frustrated—and that frustration can chip away at your confidence.

"Has anyone here had moments this week when you doubted whether you could actually write this book?"

"I sure did," said Sarah. "I was stuck in one section and felt like I was making no progress whatsoever. But now that you mention it, there were other parts of the book that went really smoothly. Still, once I hit that brick wall, I started thinking I should just give up on writing this book entirely."

"I completely understand, Sarah," said Amy. "And I'm so glad you didn't throw in the towel and that you came back to our meeting. That difficult section can wait. Focus on the parts that are flowing. When you return to it later, you'll have more writing experience under your belt. You'll have already accomplished so much, and that self-doubt won't feel as overwhelming."

"Thanks—that's a great idea. I was definitely feeling pretty defeated."

"I'm sure all of us have felt that way at some point. It's completely normal. That's why I encourage you to skip around and work on whatever is inspiring you at the moment. And if you still struggle with a particular section, maybe there's another way to approach it. You could interview someone and include their insights, rather than stressing over writing that part yourself.

"There's always a way around a brick wall—you don't have to keep slamming your head against it.

"Speaking of which," Amy added, "I didn't want to start with tools in our first meeting because I wanted you all to just start writing. But now, let's talk about writing tools—because using the right tool for the job can make all the difference.

"You've heard the phrase, 'There's more than one way to skin a cat,' and the same is certainly true for writing. Writing a book doesn't necessarily mean actually 'writing' unless you want it to. Let's talk about some ways each of you is working on your books, and exploring alternate options may give you some ideas that you can incorporate into your own work. Tina, how are you doing with your book?"

"Well, I figured that if I was supposed to write a book, I'd better get going with the right tools, so I went out shopping and bought this beautiful leather notebook and pen to use for writing my book."

"Great start, Tina! And how are things progressing?"

"Well, I must admit that I've been spending most of my time transferring my workshop notes from my computer into my new notebook but haven't actually written anything new yet. I feel like I already have writer's cramp in my hand, but no actual progress."

"I love that you got started with your book project by buying a new notebook and pen, and as a stationery lover myself, I'm all about having nice writing tools. But it seems like you're wasting a lot of time by writing your notes in your computer and then copying them to your notebook. Why not keep them on your computer and use your notebook only for brainstorming or adding to your ideas? Ultimately, you'll need a digital version of your book, meaning you're currently moving content from computer to paper and will need to reverse that process later."

"Of course! I should have realized that! Now I can see what an enormous waste of time it's been, but I love feeling as if I can sit at the beach or something, writing my book with a fancy pen."

"I love that image! How about if you sectioned off your notebook into different sections—aligned with your workshops—and perhaps wrote just the headings down? That way, you can carry your notebook for when inspiration strikes without rewriting existing notes. And perhaps you can even print out and tape into your notebook an outline of your workshop or other needed pages. A notebook doesn't need to be 100% handwritten to be beautiful!"

"You're right—I had a vision of writing by hand, but I am actually just throwing up my own roadblocks!"

"I feel as if I may have the opposite problem as Tina. I have been working on my book from a computer—just like I worked on my dissertation—but it's completely dry and clinical. I feel like I need to get out there into the real world and somehow write more organically if I ever want my book to have a soul and not just facts," piped in Sharon.

"There is certainly no one way to write a book, and it's a good idea to utilize a variety of methods in working on your book—whatever feels best for you. Is anyone using a different method?"

"I'm doing a lot of research into second marriages and finances," said Mark, "but while my head is swimming with facts, I'm stuck putting it into my own words. Plus, I feel like I'm at a standstill and not actually getting anything accomplished."

"When you do your research, Mark, what do you do with that information?"

"Well, I suppose I keep it somewhere in the depths of my brain, and then hopefully, it will come out in the book somehow."

"How about this," Amy began. "While you're doing your research, copy and paste the text directly into the framework of your manuscript. You already made an outline of important topics to address, so copy and paste text for each section right into your framework. If you did that, would you feel as if you were making progress?"

"Yes, I think it would. I could have my book finished in no time like that. But isn't that plagiarism?"

"Well, if you left it like that it would be, but what I'm suggesting is that you fill in your outline with text from other sources, and then when you're feeling inspired to go back and rewrite it in your own words, you already have your notes right there on the page. You could even rewrite in a different color or font so that you can easily see which sections you have completed and which still need work. Does that sound like something that will help to propel you forward?"

"Absolutely! If I saw pages already filled, I would definitely feel like things were coming together smoothly."

"Also, there is no reason everything needs to be rewritten. In fact, keeping certain items as direct quotes—and citing the source in your book—is a terrific way to add value to your book by including the words of experts, and as long as you give credit where credit is due, you're certainly not plagiarizing. Is anyone using any other tools besides a computer or a notebook?"

"I've been using the notepad app on my phone. I can speak into my phone and it automatically turns everything to text, plus I have my phone with me at all times, so I am prepared for when inspiration hits," said Sam.

"Terrific! And depending upon your phone and computer, your notes app may sync with your computer so that all of your content ends up easily on your computer. How about AI? Has anyone tried using AI to write their book?"

"Isn't that cheating?" asked Aidan.

"Not necessarily. Yes, using AI to write your entire book would definitely be cheating. However, using AI for research or for proofreading and correcting isn't cheating as much as it is timesaving."

"How can I use AI for research?" asked Sarah.

"Well, I know you're planning to write about all the royal weddings for the past century. Tell me, how are you finding out about each wedding?"

"Well, I've been going through the family tree of each royal household, and then once I find a couple, I Google them to read all about their wedding."

"And what sorts of things do you wish to learn about each wedding?"

"I created a spreadsheet to record details such as the bride and groom's names and ages, the wedding date and location, the bride's attire, the presence of attendants, and other noteworthy information. When I look up each royal wedding, I fill in the details on my spreadsheet."

"That sounds incredibly thorough ... and time-consuming!"

"It is, but I want to be sure to be consistent in what facts I am presenting."

"Did you know you could use AI for your research—and save a ton of time? Since you already have parameters set for what type of information you're seeking, you can query AI and get exactly what you're looking for."

"I never thought of that, and I'm not exactly sure how I would do that. Could you show me?"

"Absolutely," said Amy, as she shared her screen with the others online. "Here is an AI program—a free one, in fact!—and I'm going to type in the following: Please list all the royal weddings that have taken place for the past 100 years. For each royal wedding, please include the names of the bride and groom, their ages, the date of the wedding, the location of the wedding, details about what the bride wore, the names of their attendants, and 3-5 additional facts about the wedding."

"You do know that you are talking to a computer and you don't need to say 'please'—don't you?" chimed in Aidan sarcastically.

"You are so right, but I must admit I always say 'please' and 'thank you' to my computer when sending a query. Who knows—perhaps it will help! So Sarah, is there anything I missed in my query?"

"Nope—that sounds like exactly what I have been searching for. But can they really give me all of that information?"

"Well, there's only one way to find out," said Amy, as she pressed the SUBMIT button.

Instantly, text filled the computer screen, and the cursor typed line after line at a speed no human could match. The list included each royal couple, with bullet points beneath their names detailing their ages, the date and location of the wedding, attendants, dress details, and additional notes. Literally pages and pages of details appeared within seconds.

"I can't believe this! I have literally spent hours trying to find out this information, and you found it with the click of a button!" exclaimed Sarah—who was excited but understandably annoyed with herself for wasting so much time.

Amazement filled the rest of the group. Amy asked them to each take a few moments to write down what they would like to query AI with when class was done. "AI is simply scanning their database of the web for information much faster than you or I ever could, which is how it could come up with the list of royal weddings and details for Sarah so quickly. Using AI for research is not only a time saver because it is fast, but since you can request exactly what you are looking for, you won't need to wade through extraneous information. However, as with anything, it's good practice to review all AI-generated content critically for accuracy. Just as not everything that you find on the web is true, the same holds true for AI. But by asking the right questions—and reading the answers with discernment—you can find the content for your books coming together in no time."

"We've used AI for research in class," added Sam, "but I must admit, I never thought about asking it such pointed questions in order to get lots of information quickly. I'm definitely going to come up with a list of parameters to submit to AI so that I'll have a solid list of environmental political issues to address, and I can do so with consistency."

"As wonderful as AI research may be, I do want to chat a bit about two little words that may still plague you—writer's block. Writer's block often has two major causes: either something is wrong with the book you're writing, or something is wrong with you.

When I say something is wrong with you, I don't mean in a fundamental sense—I mean that if you're under stress, physically or emotionally, many pressures in your life could interfere with your creativity. Writing, after all, is a creative act. Even if you're not writing fiction, nonfiction still requires tapping into your own creativity. And creativity needs space and time to flourish."

"And time and space are the things we are all probably lacking," snickered Aidan.

"So true," continued Amy. "But the payoffs are enormous! Foremost, prioritize your well-being. That means getting enough rest, eating well, and practicing self-care. If you're burning yourself out in other areas of your life, simply lighting a scented candle and playing mood music won't fix the problem. Taking care of yourself is always the first step. And to help to get those creative juices flowing, some writers retreat to a beach, the desert, or even a quiet park to escape distractions, relax, and reconnect with their inspiration. Of course, not everyone can fly across the country—or across the ocean—to a villa in Tuscany to write, though that does sound inspiring to me! But you can still nurture your creativity and take care of yourself at home."

"I'm in! Who wants to join me in Tuscany to write our book?" Kami asked.

"I'm all about it!" said Amy, "And if you are serious, I lead several writer's retreats to beautiful, relaxing locations each year. But sometimes, all we need is a scented candle and some mood music to create our own retreat-like atmosphere at home so that we can get our book done. Creating an environment conducive to creativity can definitely help. Some writers prefer sitting outside, while others are most inspired by a cozy fire. Some thrive on the energy of people around them—hence, the large number of writers working on laptops in cafés. Everyone is different, so experiment until you find what works best for you. Keep in mind that what helps in one scenario may not work in another. For example, if you're doing research, you might prefer sitting at a desktop computer, whereas if you're writing a deeply personal story or memoir, you may enjoy curling up by the fire with a glass of wine. If you're feeling stuck, changing your environment can go a long way."

"As a person who loves solitude, I have often wondered how those people at the coffee shop are getting anything done," said Sharon.

"And honestly," Sarah piped in, "I think I would get more done there than at home, where I am constantly distracted by laundry and dirty dishes calling my name."

"The key is to find what works for you in making your environment conducive to writing. The other common cause of writer's block is losing your way in your manuscript. I like to compare it to hiking. Imagine you're going on a beautiful hike in a national park. You park your car at the trailhead, take a selfie by the sign, and set off on a clearly marked path.

"At first, everything is obvious—you know exactly where to go. But as you get deeper into the woods, the trail fades. A mile in, you're not even sure if you're still on the path. You thought you were following a clear trail, but now you realize you're just wandering through the woods."

"That happened to me once in the parking lot of a theme park—I swear every car looked like mine, and I was sure that I remembered which exit to take out of the park to reach my car, but I was definitely wrong," Mark reminisced.

"Mark, that happened to me, too, and we had to wait until the park closed and most of the cars were gone before we could find our car," laughed Sarah.

"Many of us, when faced with this situation, push forward—sometimes getting even more lost. The best move is actually to turn back, returning to the last place where the path was clear. But because of the sunk-cost fallacy, people often think, I've already walked two miles—I can't turn back now!—and press on, despite the uncertainty.

The same thing happens in writing. Sometimes, writer's block occurs because you've lost sight of your original direction. You were moving forward with your book, but now the path isn't clear. Many writers, like lost hikers, believe they should just keep pushing through—only to hit a brick wall. Then they berate themselves for their lack of productivity, creating a vicious cycle where they feel more and more frustrated.

Sometimes, the solution is to go back. That might mean revisiting an earlier section where you felt confident or even cutting entire chapters that no longer serve the overall message. It may feel painful to discard material you've worked hard on, but it's better than forcing your way forward when you've lost your way.

By stepping back to a point where your writing felt strong and inspired, you might find a new direction—or even realize it's time for a fresh start. And while starting over may sound daunting, it's far better than trudging ahead with no clear path in sight."

"I see," responded Mark, "although I know that I've definitely felt the sunk-cost fallacy in my life at times. It isn't easy to get past that!"

"You are so right, Mark. All we can do is our best—I'm not worried! Have a great week of writing—take care of yourselves physically and emotionally—and next time, we'll talk about beginning to spread the word about your new book."

As much as Sarah enjoyed the Zoom meeting with Amy, she couldn't wait to get off the call because she was bursting at the seams. Her fingers flew over the keyboard, typing the names of all the royal brides and getting them organized. When Amy had asked about organization strategies, she expressed that whatever method worked best for Sarah was fine with her. Some people enjoyed making folders on Google Drive, others preferred working with index cards, and many used just the Notes app on their phone.

Sarah decided she liked the idea of writing her book on the Notes app, since her phone was with her at all times. This way, if inspiration struck, she could write it down right away. She created one note for general information and then separate notes for each royal bride so she could add information and links to things like their tiaras, pictures, and more. Within a few hours, her phone was bursting with notes, and she couldn't believe how much she had accomplished so quickly.

THINK ABOUT ...

In your life, would you generally consider yourself to be a pantser or a plotter? Has that served you well in life? Did you ever need to be the other because of a particular circumstance?

Do you feel comfortable speaking extemporaneously or do you prefer to use prepared notes—and perhaps even practice—when you have important things to say? Have you ever wished that you had written things down before speaking because you missed important points? Perhaps speaking to colleagues requires one method, whereas speaking to a doctor or insurance company requires a different type of preparation.

If you wish to remember something that you suddenly thought of, are you more likely to write it down or save it electronically, or do you count on your own memory? Do you have a permanent "list" for such items? Or loads of scraps of paper lying around? Does that method work for you?

6
REPURPOSING YOUR WRITING

At our next Zoom meeting, the screen buzzed with excitement as everyone dived into their books.

"I can't believe how smoothly this is going!" Mark exclaimed. "Honestly, when we started, I thought there was no way I could do this. But now, I'm seeing pages upon pages of material, and things are really coming together. I'm far from finished, of course, but it's amazing to see a table of contents and a framework take shape."

"I'm so glad you're finding the process easier than you expected," Amy said. "My goal was to make it feel like setting a GPS—you just follow the purple line on the screen to reach your destination. Now that you all have some material built up, we're going to talk about promoting your books."

"Promoting already? I've barely even started!" interjected Kami.

"That's okay! Every little bit helps, and it's never too soon to promote your new book. But before we even talk about promotion, I want to talk about repurposing—using the material you're already writing in multiple ways. A great way to promote your book is by turning parts of it into social media posts, articles, or other content. This way, you write once but use it twice—or even three or four times."

"I feel like the poster child for repurposing material," said Sam. "I'm getting more mileage out of this one paper than all of you combined."

The others chuckled in agreement.

"Promoting my book?" Aidan groaned. "I know I should post on social media—I've heard that so many times—but honestly, I have no idea what to post."

"I get it," Amy said. "Social media can feel like another job—just another thing you have no time to think about."

"Exactly!" said Aiden. "I already have enough jobs running my business and now writing a book. How can I possibly have time to sit around and think about what to post?"

"That's the thing. Your book provides the content for your social media. I'll show you today how to turn each of your book topics into social media posts so you avoid extra work. Let's start with you, Sarah. How's the book going?"

"So far, so good. I must admit, it feels like a guilty pleasure—sitting around reading about royal weddings, which I love doing anyway!"

"So, tell me, what are you finding out, and how are you organizing it into your book?"

"Well, I've structured the first half of the book around different royal weddings. I'm researching weddings from the past 300 years and keeping track of details like who got married, what the bride wore, and specifics about the cake, venue, and ceremony. I've researched everything from the lantern decorations at the wedding of the Guangxu Emperor of China in 1889 to the proxy wedding of Marie Antoinette to her brother, the Archduke Ferdinand, representing Louis, the Dauphin of France in 1770. The second half will be tips on how to make your own wedding feel more royal. I haven't decided yet whether the book will be exactly half-and-half or if I'll mix the tips in as I go. I figure I'll decide that later."

"Sounds good," Amy said. "Right now, just building up the material is key—you can refine the structure later. And I understand that posting on social media can be daunting. Your target audience is definitely out there, but you're not sure what to post, right?"

"Exactly!"

"Well, since you're doing all this research on royal weddings, why not share what you're learning?"

"You mean just post tidbits about different weddings every day?"

"Exactly! You could focus on one wedding per week and break it into daily posts—Monday, the dress; Tuesday, the cake; Wednesday, the venue, and so on. You could even create a calendar of royal wedding anniversaries and align your posts with them."

"Hey, I like that idea!" In fact, Queen Victoria's wedding anniversary is coming up. Maybe I could wish her a happy anniversary on my page and then spend the rest of the week sharing different details about her wedding."

"Perfect! That way, your page will attract people who love royalty and weddings—exactly the right audience for your book. Does that sound like too much extra work?"

"Not at all! Since I already have the material, I'd just be repurposing it. And knowing that I have posts to create will motivate me to keep my research on track."

"That's great! I'm definitely going to follow you online and see what you're posting. I recommend mixing up your content—some posts can be text-heavy, others can feature images, and some could even be short videos of you discussing royal weddings. Variety keeps people engaged. Also, be sure to use tags effectively."

"How would I use tags?"

"Even though you're talking about historical figures like Queen Victoria, you should also post about today's royals. Tag them in your posts when relevant."

"Oh, my goodness! I would die of excitement if a royal ever shared one of my posts!"

"You have to start somewhere! So, yes, post about past royal weddings but also share and comment on current royal news. If you want to be known as a 'royal specialist,' your content should reflect that."

"Well, goodness knows I keep up with royal news!"

"I figured you did. And for those posts, you don't even have to write much—just re-share news articles with a brief comment."

"I love the royal family, too!" Sharon chimed in. "I'm definitely going to follow your page to keep up with the latest royal news."

"This sounds like so much fun," Sarah said. "Not like another job—more like turning my guilty pleasure into work."

"I wish my social media strategy was that easy," Sharon said. "Somehow, chemistry doesn't make the news as much as royalty."

"That's okay!" Amy reassured her. "I'm sure we can find a way to spin it. First, tell us how your book is going and what you're focusing on."

"Well, we were talking about food chemistry, and that's sparked my interest in cooking. I've been experimenting in the kitchen so I can explain chemical reactions and how understanding them can help people make their food taste better."

"That sounds fantastic!" Amy said. "Honestly, that sounds like exactly what I'd want to see on your social media feeds."

"But what would I post?" Sharon asked. "I think the book is coming along well, but I'm not sure how interesting it is in small bites."

"How about recipes?" Kami suggested. "There are plenty online that you could share. If you focus on a particular chemical reaction each week, you could start with an explanation and then follow it up with a week's worth of recipes that highlight that reaction."

"That actually sounds fun," Sharon said. "Do I have to write all the recipes myself?"

"Not at all! You can share existing recipes and tag the original creators. When you tag others, their followers may see your post, which helps build your own audience."

"That definitely doesn't sound overwhelming," Sharon admitted.

"As the resident chemist," Aidan said, "I'd think there are also news stories you could comment on—things like chemical spills, new medications, or even scientific breakthroughs."

"Good point!" said Amy. "And the same goes for those of you in real estate or construction. If the tallest skyscraper in the world is being built in Abu Dhabi, that's worth sharing, even if you're not involved in the project. Trending topics help your posts reach more people."

"Well," Sarah laughed, "the royals get into the news often enough—sometimes not for the best reasons!"

"Exactly!" Amy said. "You've got plenty of material to work with."

"What should I be posting?" asked Mark. "According to my brokerage firm, I'm not supposed to be giving financial advice online, so I don't want to cross any lines."

"That's understandable. But remember that people do business with people that they know and trust. Thus, your goal on social media should be to become likable—a person who others feel as if they know. Of course, how personal you get is entirely up to you. While some professionals share their families and out-of-office lives more freely, others have definite boundaries in place. Either approach can work, but it's good to decide where your line-in-the-sand will lie. For example, Mark, you're targeting to work with single parents and second marriages, which is a demographic you belong to. Do you feel comfortable sharing your family online so that people will know that you are in a blended family?"

"Well, I do occasionally post pictures of my kids and wife, and my ex and I get along now. In fact, we're planning our daughter's Sweet 16 together so that both sides of the family will be present. Is that what you mean?"

"Exactly! In the past you may have simply posted a ball game or family gathering, but if you also mention—either in the same post or in other posts—that you're blending families together, your followers will begin to realize that you understand their own situations more personally than they may have realized, and you'll become top-of-mind for themselves and their referrals in considering financial planning for second families."

"Got it. Also, while I can't give financial advice, that also helps me to understand what other items I can post—or repost—in order to build my following. Are there other ways to target that demographic online?"

"You could join groups that contain your target market, as well. For example, I'm in a pickleball-lover's group online, and I'll bet that if I were a physical therapist dealing with pickleball injuries, that would be the perfect place to meet people," chimed in Kami.

"Sounds good—but isn't it a bit heavy-handed to solicit customers in a group like that?"

"It can be, and many groups have rules against personal promotions. However, if your online profile image and page talk about what you do and people check you out because you are part of interesting conversations and posts online, you aren't breaking any rules or taboos. Instead, you are building community and widening your circle of potential referrals."

"There aren't any groups for couples about to split up, are there?" asked Tina. "Come to think of it, that would actually be hilarious!"

"None that I have ever seen, although with the divorce rate so high, I suppose all groups are filled with potential clients."

"Well, if that is true, what should I be doing online? Unlike Mark, I am still married to my college boyfriend."

"Lucky you! Just be yourself and be approachable," answered Amy. "Remember that people work with others they know and like, so even though you aren't necessarily a member of your target market, the fact is if you value family and relationships, post about that, and people will view you as the marriage counselor who actually wants to help—not the one who wishes to deliver the divorce papers. And tell me, don't most people who seek marriage counseling want to make it work on some level?"

"You would think that, but often only one person wants to make it work, and they drag the other along. But now that I think about it, it's the person who wants it to work who actually calls me and makes the appointment, so I suppose that appealing to the optimists isn't necessarily a bad idea after all! And not only do I have plenty of tips to share, I have some wild stories, as well."

"So, essentially our goals on social media should be twofold—you want to establish a personal connection so that people want to work with you and refer you to others, and you want to post about your areas of expertise so that you can not only build community but also so that people who may know you personally but not know what you do would learn more about you. Most of you likely have a wide circle of connections on social media already, and whether they're cousins or car pool parents, I would bet that many of them have no idea what you do. They're already seeing many of your posts naturally, so if they see you are involved in an area that they either need or could refer to, since they already have a personal relationship with you, you would likely get them as a client."

"I can see how that definitely works," Sharon chimed in. "I once posted a picture from a faculty event at the university, and a relative I rarely see contacted me and asked if I could help get her daughter accepted as a student. While this may not have been something that brought me any personal benefit, the fact is they saw the post, didn't know previously that I was a professor, and they contacted me."

"Exactly! And the same can happen for Kami or Aidan if someone needed to sell or fix their house—provided they're in the right location."

"I must admit, I don't see relatives calling me for marriage counseling," Tina laughed.

"True, but while I don't see cousins calling me for financial advice either, perhaps they would refer me to others."

"That's true, Mark, but for both of you, it could even be that a business organization is looking for a speaker, and because you were top of mind from seeing your posts, they called you."

"I'm glad that I am in a photo-driven field so that I can post pictures of listings easily."

"That's very true. And since you're doing a collaborative book, Kami, you could also introduce and tag your collaborators on social media. This online promotion will delight your collaborators and remind them to promote you in return. If you're looking to build referral partners, posting regularly about the other professionals in your book will help you to more easily refer them to your connections, and vice versa."

"I'm not seeing that my posting about international environmental issues can possibly lead to anything lucrative for me," said Sam.

"Not true! Just as there was someone in my own circle who didn't know that I was a chemistry professor and then asked me for help with their kid getting into college, you never know who might be in your own circle of connections. Now that we are talking about it, I realize that I have a friend who is an international lawyer based in London. Would that be someone who would be a valuable introduction for you?"

"Could be—I'd love to meet them!"

"Wonderful—give me your email address in the chat window, and I'll send an introductory email later today."

"Wow—we are benefiting before even posting!" laughed Amy. "I can only imagine the benefits once you get going. So this week, get started posting—even if they are simply casual, friendly posts—and be sure to find a way to mention your area of expertise. Next, you will want to more regularly find material from your book that you can share online, or even repost items of interest that you find that tie in with your topic area. And finally, tag others in your posts, as doing so will both increase the visibility of your posts to a whole new audience and build connections with others one by one. Also, connect with me and other group members on social media so we can like, comment, and share your posts to increase their reach. I will email a list of social media links and handles for you to connect with from our group. Happy posting!"

After the meeting, Sarah sat down to tackle her social media accounts and make a plan.

This is so helpful because I never know what to post on social media about my business, thought Sarah. *Certainly, when I am having a wedding, I know to post about it, but even then I have to wait until the bride okays it. This is a great way for me to have something to post even in between weddings.*

Sarah dove right in and discovered that one of her favorite royal brides was going to be celebrating their anniversary in just a few days. "Well, she will be my bride for the week!" Sarah exclaimed. "Every day, I will have a different post about the wedding, culminating in the wedding picture on the actual anniversary."

She set up the posts—one for each day—talking about the princess's bouquet, tiara, dress, and wedding cake, with the royal picture and best wishes for a happy anniversary on the actual anniversary day. She tagged many of the wedding vendors she had met in her business, as well as important terms like "bridal" and "wedding planning." Finally, she thought, *Why not?* and tagged #TheRoyalFamily.

Perhaps nothing will come of it, but it's certainly worth trying, Sarah thought.

She hadn't felt this excited about her business since she opened her doors six months ago. Even dealing with those difficult brides and weddings, which were her current clients, didn't seem so ominous now that she had a plan in place to secure better clients for the future.

At their check-in call, Sarah could hardly wait to show Amy how much progress she had made, but Amy wasn't surprised a bit.

"Goodness, Sarah, you've been busy! I followed you on Instagram, and I am absolutely loving what you're doing with the royal brides. And I see you're attracting quite a following already—you're certainly not the only one who adores European royalty!"

Sarah was thrilled. As much as she was excited about the idea of focusing her business on royal weddings, she was admittedly a bit concerned that it was too narrow a field. But seeing how many people were loving the posts was making her feel much better about her choice.

"Even if just a small percentage of all those people who love royalty called me—or even if they simply shared with their friends that they knew an expert when the time came—I would be over the moon!" Sarah exclaimed.

"One step at a time," said Amy. "Not to worry, we will get there."

THINK ABOUT ...

People have understandably mixed feelings when it comes to social media mixing personal lives and business together. Some are concerned that they will look too sales-y, while still others are worried that once their networks expand to include more and more business contacts, they will feel less comfortable sharing personal details and photos from their life. These are completely valid concerns, and thinking about your own personal boundaries before diving in is a prudent course of action.

For example, while some people think nothing of sharing baby photos and children's accomplishments, others would feel that is clearly past their comfort level. And while there are ways to separate groups on social media for posting, the chances of their being a slip-up are likely, so the classic advice of not posting something you're uncomfortable with everyone seeing is probably a good place to start. What are your own boundaries? Think ahead to decide how you will treat different events and people on social media so that you have a plan in place.

And even if you don't want to share your family with the world, there are other ways for you to appear accessible and friendly and build relationships online. For example, one may enjoy pickleball, rom-coms, and fabulous food, and sharing some of those items makes others feel personally connected with no boundaries being crossed. What are some interests or areas that you may wish to share online comfortably?

7
MEETING YOUR AUDIENCE'S EXPECTATIONS

"For today, what I would really like to focus on is your book cover and title." Amy explained that once they had a cover and title in place, everyone could actually begin posting about their upcoming book. "The primary goals of your title and cover are to attract readers—the right readers—and to give potential readers an idea of what your book is about. For example, on the one hand, Aidan's book could have tools for construction on the cover, or it could have an incredibly gory picture of a person after a chainsaw accident. One of those books would look like a 'how-to' book, while the other would look like a slasher novel. You want to ensure that your book cover and title effectively establish the stage to meet your audience's expectations positively and avoid misleading or confusing potential readers to prevent disappointment.

"Sarah, you're attracting quite a following already, and I certainly want all of those followers to know that something exciting—your book—is in the works. So tell us, when you picture your book, what does it look like? Do you see an actual photo of a royal bride? Or maybe a beautiful tiara intertwined with flowers and a castle in the background?"

Sarah thought about it. "I think I prefer the thought of the tiara rather than an actual photograph so that I don't limit myself to picking just one royal bride."

"Makes sense to me. And what about a title? Have you given any thought to what the title of your book might be?"

"I've been giving an awful lot of thought to it. I really want to be sure that my readers know it's not just a book about royal weddings, but that they can have their own royal weddings. I don't want people to think that royal weddings are just, well, for royalty—they can be for all of us, and I can help make that happen."

"You are so right. How about a title like *Your Royal Wedding*? And then in the subtitle, we can put something like *Learn from Royal Brides to Create Your Own Royal Wedding*."

"I like the sound of that!" said Sarah.

"Remember, everyone—your book cover has just one job, to draw in readers. If your book was in a store, the entire role of the book cover is to make people pick up your book. If your book is online, the action we want people to take is to click on it. So we want to be sure that your book cover is enticing, but for the right crowd. Kami, have you given any thought to your cover?"

"I guess you're going to tell me I should have a 'For Sale' sign on my cover?"

"Absolutely! But unlike Sarah's cover, I think you should be in the picture, too—so that people can see you next to the 'For Sale' sign. With Sarah's cover, the focus is on royal brides—

and how you can become one yourself. In real estate, people are much more personal with their agent, and so having you on the cover makes sense. Am I right in guessing that your picture is on your business card?"

"You guessed right! And so a book with my picture would actually be a great way to boost my brand and have people think of the two items together."

"Exactly! Sarah, am I correct in guessing that your picture is not on your business card?"

"Correct! Right now I have a rather generic wedding clip art on my business card. But I certainly realize that I want to brand myself to match my book, too. While I've been working on my book and social media to focus on royal weddings, my business card and logo still look like a generic wedding planning business. I am definitely going to change that right away!"

"Fabulous! For all of us here, the goal isn't just to publish a book—it's to ignite your business. That could mean anything from collaborating with great referral partners like Kami is doing to laser-focusing your target market like Sarah. Yes, we want to finish with a book-in-hand, but more importantly, we want to be on our way to a more profitable and personally fulfilling business than we had before."

"What will be on my book cover—bags of money?" asked Mark.

"One of the best ways to think about what you want for the cover of your book is to look at similar-topic books in a bookstore or on Amazon. Since we're on Zoom, I'm going to share my screen and put financial planning into the search bar to see what we find there."

MEETING YOUR AUDIENCE'S EXPECTATIONS

Amy shared her screen, and after she put in the search term a whole screen filled up with oddly similar looking books.

"What do you see in common with these covers, Mark?"

"Well, all of them have big text and a picture of the author."

"Great observations—anyone else?"

"They seem to have quite a bit of text—much more than just a two-word title." "And the text is in a primary color." "And the author appears wealthy—or at least well put together." "And all the book covers are white."

"Wow—fantastic observations! There seems to be a strong similarity between all the best-selling books in this category. What do you think that means?"

"That the authors are all boring and uncreative?" Aidan joked, added his two-cents.

"While that may be true, it also means that readers have an expectation of what the best-selling books in this category look like. If there was a book cover that looked different on this page, what do you think readers would think?"

"Well, I guess if I was in a bookstore and there was a book that looked different from these, I might think they put it in the wrong place."

"Exactly! There's an old saying that you should dress for the job you want, and the same goes for book covers. Think about where in a bookstore—what section and shelf—you would like to find your book, and then look at the covers of the best-selling books that are already there. You want your book to emulate the best sellers in your category so that potential readers see it as belonging and being in the right place.

"Is everything okay, Sharon? You've been awfully quiet today." Amy suddenly realized that while most had been rather animated during the Zoom meeting, Sharon hadn't said a word.

"Well, I must admit that I'm a bit jealous of everyone making such substantial progress with their books, while I feel like I'm at a complete loss."

"Wow, I'm glad I asked! That explains a lot. What's going on? Is it writer's block, or are you struggling with your message?"

"To be honest, I feel like I don't even like my book very much. In the beginning, the concept—tying chemistry with cooking—sounded like a great idea. But as I started posting about it online, I realized that cooking doesn't genuinely interest me as much as I thought. I don't feel like I fit in with the cooking communities online. If I can't fit in there and don't really enjoy the topic, I feel completely lost. I feel like a total failure."

"You're not a failure," said Sarah. "If anything, I think it's great that you realized this before you got in too deep."

"You don't think I'm already in too deep?" Sharon asked. "I feel like all of you are way ahead of me, and I'm still standing at the starting line—except now, I've decided I don't even like my sneakers!"

"It's never too late," said Kami. "Isn't that right, Amy? Isn't it better that she realized this now instead of later?"

"Absolutely! It's never too late, and this is such an insightful realization. You're right—if you don't like the community and don't feel a connection, it probably isn't the right place for you. So let's rewind a bit to when we first talked about your book. Let's go back to why you're writing it in the first place."

MEETING YOUR AUDIENCE'S EXPECTATIONS

"Well, I need to write a book to gain tenure at the university. I suppose I could focus on some boring chemical topic and write a dissertation like last time, but I was really hoping for something with a little more zip."

"When you say zip, what does that mean to you?"

"Well, while I love my position at the university, I'd love to be more relevant to people outside of academia. I hear you all talking about posting on social media, guesting on podcasts, and leading workshops, and I absolutely love the sound of that. But I'm sure some boring topic on chemicals isn't going to get me invited onto a podcast or asked to lead a workshop.

"We all talked about the chemistry-cooking connection, and it seemed like a good way to make chemistry more accessible to the average person. But while I do enjoy cooking a bit at home, hanging out with a bunch of chefs online doesn't sound fun to me."

"Well, you've got all of us here to brainstorm other possible topics. Does anyone have any suggestions?"

"Would something like chemistry and medicine interest you?" asked Sam. "For example, I have no idea what's actually in the pills I take or why they work."

"That's an idea," said Sharon, "although I must admit, I have a total aversion to blood, and the thought of anything medical is probably as foreign to me as chemistry is to you!"

"How about chemistry and construction?" asked Aidan.

"What do you mean?"

"Well, I was thinking about materials like paint thinner,

bleach, and other chemicals used in construction—how they work, when to use them, and how to stay safe."

"I suppose there's a connection there, but I'm not very handy with construction materials, so I'm probably not the best person for that book, either. After so many years in chemistry, you'd think I would know something about a topic I actually want to write about!"

"Well, you're not just looking for any topic—you already know plenty about chemistry as an academic subject. What we're hoping to find is a topic with mainstream appeal. Any other ideas?"

"How about wine or beer?" Kami chimed in. "I was just at a winery over the weekend, and on the tour, they talked about all sorts of chemical processes. I had no idea what they were saying, but I bet you would understand it."

"Well, I certainly like wine," Sharon said, laughing. "And this book project is definitely driving me to drink! That might be a fabulous topic. I'm just not sure what my angle should be."

"How about what makes wines different from each other?"

"If I knew there was a scientific reason for why things taste the way they do, I'd feel more confident trying new wines instead of feeling like I'm just taking a gamble."

"Or how wine and food pair well—or badly—together?"

"Or why I get a headache drinking Chardonnay but not Pinot Grigio?"

All at once, everyone was excitedly peppering Sharon with their questions about wine.

"Wow! These all sound like something I'd love to research. And I bet posting in wine-drinking forums would be much more fun than posting in cooking forums. Can I really do that? Can I change course like this?"

"Absolutely," said Amy. "Even if you were one paragraph from the end of writing your book, you could still change course. But since it sounds like you're still at the starting line, this is the perfect time. And remember—your book is just one piece of the puzzle. Our goal is for your book to become the cornerstone of your brand. Would you rather build your brand around food or wine?"

"Oh, wine for sure! I can already picture myself leading workshops, giving talks, and—heck—maybe even running a wine tour of Italy!"

"I love the way you think," said Kami. "Sign me up!"

"So, since we're going back to the beginning with your book, let's revisit the concepts of goals, target audience, and structure. It sounds like you've already nailed down your goals and have a lot of feedback on your target audience. That's great! What about book structure? We talked about the eight main types of book structures a few weeks back. Does anyone have thoughts on what might be a good fit for Sharon's wine book?"

"Since she's starting on a fresh path, would it be a good idea for her to collaborate with experts? Even if it's not the entire book, getting insights from others could be really helpful."

"That sounds great! And I'd love to meet people in the industry. What kind of experts are we talking about? Sommeliers? Winery owners?"

"I don't know much about chemistry, but I wouldn't be surprised if even the grape growers or farmers played a big role in how wine turns out. Instead of giving each expert their own chapter, you could weave in their insights through interviews or citations."

"If I were starting a book from scratch, I think I'd want a very structured approach—maybe something like an A-to-Z guide," Mark suggested. "I feel like that would help everything come together more easily."

"I think you're right, Mark. While I'm not sure I could find something for every letter of the alphabet, I do think structure is key. I'm mulling over whether I should organize the book by wine types—red, white, sparkling—by regions where the grapes are grown, or by something else entirely."

"You could do both," said Amy. "I can almost picture it: the first section of your book could be about the growing process and wine production. Then, part two could have different chapters based on the types of wines and how they taste, along with food pairings and such. I can send you a sample structure like I did before—would you like that?"

"I'd love that! Although, to be honest, this book already feels so much more like me than my last one. I feel like I could write the whole thing tonight! Well, maybe not tonight, but I'm so glad the university is closed for vacation next week—I can't wait to get started!"

"That's great! I love seeing you this excited!"

"And don't worry about me holding us all back," said Sharon. "I'm literally taking notes as we chat, and I'm already brainstorming titles and cover ideas. This is going to be great!"

"Well, don't worry about slowing us down—it sounds like we'll be trying to catch up to you in no time!"

"The only thing I think I'll hold off on—at least for now—is posting on social media. I don't want to go in the wrong direction again like I did with the food topic. This time, since I truly believe in the concept, I want to make sure my first impression online is a strong one."

"Makes sense to me. And when you're ready, you can always deactivate your old posts and start fresh. Just be sure to connect with all of us when you do—we'll shower your posts with activity!"

"Thank you so much! I feel so supported here—you have no idea!"

THINK ABOUT …

Look through the books you own and focus on the covers. Can you tell what type of book each is from its cover? If the title text were in another language, would you still be able to tell what the book was about? If not, would that hinder you in buying that book?

Next, head over to a bookstore—either in person or online—and find the section where you would like your book to appear. While you may not find any exactly like yours, you want to find those that would appeal to the same reader as your book. Look at the book covers and focus on the similarities you are seeing. You'll want your book to look, ideally, like it belongs with the others.

Of course, these are general rules of thumb, and if you have a specific vision for your book cover that differs radically from the norm, it's your book and your creative vision. Be aware that you may need to attract your audience in other ways, which, while certainly possible, may introduce a hindrance in positioning your book.

8
BOOK DESCRIPTION AND PITCH

Sarah had never been busier with work—not only was she spending time researching and writing her book, but she was also crafting graphics and posts to share information online, mulling over cover ideas, and making time for two potential client meetings with people who called her because they found her online. Her new book wasn't even finished yet—heck, she hadn't even totally committed to a title!—and yet this book project was bringing her new business. She couldn't be happier, even when Ryan teased they were having pizza for the third night in a row.

"I knew you could do it, Sarah, but honestly, I'm amazed at how quickly your book is coming together." Ryan was truly surprised, thinking the finished book would be years in the making.

"I must admit that I'm shocked, too. I was afraid I couldn't do it, and here I am already getting new clients because of a book that isn't even finished yet. Amazing!"

Sarah was looking forward to their next group meeting—both to keep moving ahead with her book, and to find out if Sharon's new wine book was coming along.

"So nice to see everyone," Amy started the Zoom meeting. "Let's begin with wins and challenges. Does anyone have a success they would like to share with the group or a challenge you may need some assistance with?"

Sarah was already bursting at the seams to share. "I had two potential clients call this week because they found me on social media. That has never happened before!"

"That's fantastic news! I know you had been essentially taking any clients that came your way, but once your phone is ringing more regularly, you can certainly afford to be picky."

"I was thinking the same thing. I've already rewritten my contract, so it clearly states that I'm not responsible for spontaneous childcare."

"Good thinking, Sarah. I never thought about specifying what I won't do in a contract. I think I may look at my own contract this week and see what I can firm up," added Mark.

"Any other wins or challenges to share?" asked Amy.

"Well, I can't top two new clients, but I do feel as if my couples' workshop is really starting to take shape. Thinking about the book as a framework for the workshop—and vice versa—has really helped me to get my notes organized into topics and sections. I'm completing two projects at once—my book and my workshop presentations—which is a huge bonus and makes my time very well spent."

"I feel the same way about my business. Before, I would just go to networking meetings and such hoping to meet someone looking for financial services, but now I have something targeted to say, and I feel like more people are asking me questions and showing an interest in what I'm doing."

"Sharon, how are things going with you and the new direction you're taking?"

"Well, as excited as I was leaving our last meeting, I must admit that I spent half the week having anxiety about throwing away hours and hours of work." Everyone laughed knowingly. "But once I resigned myself to the lost time, I found that the new direction was much more inspiring, and I was feeling like I could envision the next steps as far as talks and workshops. But I must admit, while Sarah is making more money because of her book, I am spending more since it seems fitting to always be drinking expensive wine while working on a book about wine!"

"Well, if you ever want a wine buddy to write with, feel free to call me!" Tina offered.

"I second that! And while I've made no money from this book yet, I definitely feel possibilities in the air as I have been meeting with potential contributors and referral partners. I've already connected with a terrific real estate attorney and home inspector."

"I'm loving hearing all of these possibilities in the air. Today we are discussing book descriptions and book pitches. You'll find that sometimes the fewer words you are writing, the more difficult it can be. However, the relatively small amount of words in your book description and pitch will probably be more important than most of the words in your book.

"We spoke about how the main purpose of your book cover and title is to make the casual browser pick up or click on your book. Once someone does that, what is the very next action they take?"

"I suppose if I am in a bookstore and a book looks interesting to me, I'll pick it up and then flip it over to read the back cover," answered Mark.

"Exactly! And what about if you see a book online—what action do you take?"

"Well, if I'm online and something appeals to me, I'll click on it so that I can get more information," added Sharon.

"And what you will see on the details page is essentially the same as what you would see on the back of the book if it were in your hand. What sorts of things would you expect to read there? And what could you see would entice you to purchase the book?"

"Well, I suppose I would want to make sure that the book is what I was looking for—that it answers any questions I may have, and that it sounds like a book that I would enjoy reading," answered Mark.

"What else may help push you toward a purchase as you're reading the back of a book?" asked Amy.

"I like when unfamiliar things compare themselves to something I might already know. For example, a new TV show might say, 'If you liked *Game of Thrones*, you'll love *House of the Dragon*,' or something like that. Travel destinations often use the same approach—like 'If you like Aruba, then you'll love the Maldives.' Comparisons make it easier to relate to and get excited about something new."

"And I enjoy reading reviews—like what other people have said about a product, show, or movie," added Sharon.

"These are all valuable insights, and thinking about them will help you craft a book description that helps to turn shoppers into buyers. I will send you each a template—like a blank framework for you to fill out in order to craft your perfect book description. The most important thing that your book description must do is to address the question foremost in a potential reader's mind. You want your reader to see that you can tell what they're thinking, and that your book will answer their questions and effectively solve their problems. For example, Sarah's book is about planning your own royal wedding. What do we think is the #1 question on a potential reader's mind? And what problem do you think they need addressed?"

"I think that someone who sees Sarah's book is wondering 'How can I plan my own royal wedding,' and their biggest problem is that they don't have millions of dollars," answered Kami.

"Good thinking! Can anyone think of any other questions or problems a potential reader may want to know?"

"How about 'What actually makes a royal wedding royal?'" added Sharon.

"That's a great one. Any others?"

"I'd love to know specifics—like what types of flowers royal brides would use—and things like that," added Kami.

"These are great, Sarah. Do you have anything to add?"

"These sound like what I am including in the book already. So are you saying that I want to make sure that my book description mentions these items?" asked Sarah.

"Exactly! Your book description can say something like: Plan your own royal wedding—from flowers to food and everything in between. Or, learn what royal brides have included in their own weddings, and how to replicate the look for less."

"And perhaps I can even add some fun details, like: Find out why Queen Victoria was the first bride to wear white or something enticing like that."

"That would be terrific, and after addressing their key questions, you can do your 'comparison' line, something like: If you love *Bridgerton* or follow the royal families, you'll want your wedding to be fit for nobility!"

"That would certainly make me want to buy your book, Sarah," added Kami. "But what problem or question am I addressing in my book? Since I have various contributors, I feel like I have multiple issues to address."

"And you could certainly address them all in your book description, or at least the highlights. Something like: Are you thinking of buying or selling your home and are overwhelmed by all the things you don't know? Read on, and learn from experts all about selecting a real estate agent. Do you need title insurance? Is a home inspection necessary? What are 'points?' And so much more!"

"Oh, yes! Could my comparison line mention a TV show—like something on HGTV?" asked Kami.

"It certainly could. You do want your comparison line to appeal to your target buyer. If your target buyer watches HGTV, then it's a good fit. However, if you're targeting a different type of buyer—for example, men or older people— then you'll want to check if those demographics are HGTV watchers."

"Makes sense to me—I'm on it!" exclaimed Kami.

"I'm not sure I understand what question my potential readers may ask themselves," said Mark. "But they sure do have a problem to solve—growing and protecting their assets after a divorce."

"Well, if that's their problem, then the big question to be answered is: 'How can I grow and protect my assets after a divorce?' Can anyone think of other questions a reader of Mark's book might have?"

"How about 'What financial considerations should I keep in mind before filing for divorce?'"

"Or how about the more optimistic version of that same question: 'What financial considerations should I keep in mind before getting remarried?'"

"And 'How do I ensure my own children's financial protection in a blended family?'"

"These are all great questions. Mark, are these the very topics you're covering in your book?"

"Exactly! These plus more about different scenarios that could occur. So I should put these types of questions on the back of my book?"

"Yes, because if a person is reading a book description and it sounds like the author can read their mind—like they know exactly what the reader is thinking—then the reader will want to buy the book because they can tell that the author understands their concerns and that the book will solve their problems."

"All of you have potential readers with actual problems, but my potential readers don't have a problem. What do I do then?" asked Sharon.

"While it may not seem like a problem—like a life-or-death issue—your potential readers certainly have questions. What types of questions do any of us have when we see a book about wine written by a chemist?"

"Well, I love wine and would love to know if there are scientific reasons certain types of wine taste the way they do. That could help me choose new wines more easily."

"And I sometimes get a headache when I drink wine—I'd love to know if there is a chemical reason for it and what I should avoid."

"I'd be curious if there was an actual reason some wines pair better with some foods, or if it was just a matter of taste."

"These are great questions," Amy responded. "I think they all describe a person who wants tangible knowledge so that they can be more confident wine drinkers and buyers. While it might not be as important a concern as something about a person's financial stability, people certainly want to know more to avoid wasting money."

"That makes sense to me, and it definitely gives me a much better idea of what to include on the back of a book. Is it OK to start a book description with a question, like 'Have you ever wondered why you're drawn to certain wines?' or 'Does choosing a bottle feel like a guessing game every time?'" Sharon asked.

"Asking a question is a fabulous way to start a book description, and you can follow it with either more questions or perhaps a few bullet points addressing some of the subsections you'll discuss, such as food pairings, headaches, and shopping tips," Amy added. "And if you don't have something like a book or movie for your comparison statement, you can say something like 'Learn to select wines like the head sommelier at a five-star Michelin restaurant' or words to that effect."

"I like that," piped in Mark. "I'm thinking that a sentence like that—but perhaps swapping in 'top financial planners and multi-millionaires' might be what my future readers are looking for."

"Sounds good," said Amy. "The goal is for potential readers to see themselves in your book description—for them to feel as if you are speaking directly to their own questions, fears, and needs, and thus choosing your book is an absolute no-brainer, as it is exactly what they're looking for. After this meeting, I'd like each of you to work on your book description, being sure to include the questions or concerns your readers already have, a comparison statement, and perhaps even social proof in the manner of reviews from others, if possible. Following the template, you'll be able to craft a description that entices and encourages potential buyers to become readers."

"Do my readers have a problem to solve? I thought that I was the one with the problem—and my problem is getting into grad school!" Sam exclaimed.

"Very true, but while your goal may be getting into grad school, your reader's problem is that they don't understand how environmental issues affect the politics of an area. You're solving their problem—their lack of knowledge—by giving them clarity and understanding."

"Oh, I get it! So while their problem isn't a broken marriage or even how to choose the right wine, a lack of knowledge and understanding is a problem in itself."

"Exactly! You may be solving a problem that the reader doesn't even know they have, as people lacking knowledge rarely know it unless you mention something that makes them think, 'That sounds interesting—I didn't know that!'

"So while the main function of a book description is to tell the potential readers what your book is about, you also want to entice the reader with comparison statements, reviews, and questions that get into the reader's mind so that they realize you understand their concerns and that your book will address them.

"On a slightly different note, I also want to speak to everyone today about your book pitch. There will be many times when people will ask you what your book is about. You might be at a party, a guest on a podcast, or even on line in a store when someone says, 'I heard you wrote a book—what is it about?' and it is important that you can answer in a succinct yet enticing manner."

"So should we write our book description and then memorize it for such occasions?" asked Kami.

"Not exactly," Amy replied, "since your book description will probably be something that is better read with the eyes than said aloud. But also, you'll want something shorter than your full description—something easily woven into conversation. Many times, it will be just one sentence, derived from your book description opening sentence when you state what problem your book solves. So, I'd like you to take a moment to think about how you will answer the question, 'So, what is your book about?' in a way that is succinct and appealing."

"Well, my book description will start with something like: *Plan your own royal wedding—from flowers to food and everything in between—and learn what royal brides have included in their own weddings and how to replicate the look for less,* so if I turned it around to answer the question, 'What is your book about?' I suppose I could say that my book is about planning your wedding to be like a royal wedding but accessible to all. Is that what you mean by a pitch?"

"Exactly!" exclaimed Amy. "You'd be shocked by how many people I meet and ask, 'What's your book about?' and honestly, their answer is so disjointed and long-winded that I have absolutely no desire to read it. Sharon, what can you say to answer the question, 'What is your book about?'"

"How about: *My book explains the chemistry of wine production, helping wine-lovers make intelligent wine and food choices based on scientific facts*?"

"Sounds good! And you can certainly weave that statement into conversation with others without missing a beat. Kami, how about you?"

"What if I said that my book is *a collection of real estate professionals speaking about various issues that a home buyer may encounter*?"

"That would be great, or you could leave out the fact that it is a collection, and instead say that it is *a guide to real estate for seniors—from downsizing and selling to negotiating terms on your new place.* So this week, you'll be working on your book description as well as your book pitch—with your description being longer and helping to convince the potential reader to buy your book, and your book pitch being much shorter and its purpose is to answer the conversational question, 'What is your book about?' Good luck everyone!"

THINK ABOUT ...

When you meet new people—whether at a party or a networking event—they likely ask similar questions once they hear your answer to the opening line, "So what do you do?" Re-enact that social interaction in your mind and listen to the questions people ask you. Now, formulate answers to those questions—preparing you for when they inevitably arise—ensuring your responses present you and your business favorably, inspiring the questioner to want to work with you and your company.

Now roll back that social interaction to your answer to the question, "So what do you do?" Think about how your answer to that question can put you and your business in a favorable light right off the bat, before the conversation has progressed any further.

If possible, formulate your answer to that initial question—"So what do you do?"—to include the answers (or at least the inclusion of the questions) you are likely to be asked next. Demonstrating that you already know what is on a person's mind helps to build instant trust and credibility in an interaction that previously would have been simply an exchange of basic information.

9
PATHS TO PUBLICATION

Over the next couple of weeks, Sarah worked hard on her new book, continued posting content and growing her audience online, and onboarding new clients who had connected with her. She also reworked her own business documents and workflow to better reflect the focused direction she was taking her business. Each member of the group sent updates to Amy about their own progress, and she sent back suggestions and guidance to keep their book projects moving forward. Sarah felt as if she had a new circle of friends, and as she saw them daily online, she would comment, like, and share their posts in order to help them get more views and build their own circle of influence.

At the next online meeting, Sarah felt as if she were catching up with old friends. "Well, since everyone has been making such significant progress with their books, today we're going to talk about publication. Does anybody know what it actually means to publish?" Amy asked.

"Well, I guess when something gets published, like a book or an article, it means that it's placed someplace," Kami responded.

"Exactly. To publish honestly just means to make public. So, if you put a post on LinkedIn or something, you're actually publishing that post. Now, when it comes to books, we often think that publishing means somebody else is responsible for getting the book out into the world. But just as you can post something on LinkedIn yourself, you can also self-publish your book. Of course, there are many more steps to self-publishing a book than simply putting up a post on social media."

"I've heard about self-publishing," said Kami. "But isn't that what someone does when they can't get a publisher?"

"That used to be true," Amy said. "In fact, the very first self-published books were ones that couldn't find a traditional publisher for various reasons. In those cases, the author would self-publish their book, sometimes even printing copies themselves at home. Beatrix Potter's book *The Tale of Peter Rabbit* was self-published, as were *Fifty Shades of Grey* and Julia Child's *The Joy of Cooking*. Fortunately, nowadays, even if you choose to self-publish, you don't have to have a printing press in your house."

"That's good," said Sarah. "I don't think I have that much room!"

Everyone chuckled.

"But why wouldn't someone be able to find a publisher?" Mark asked. "Don't publishers want to publish books?"

"That would make sense," Amy said. "And there are different types of publishers, so it's certainly possible to find one if you're interested. But back in the day, there were far fewer publishers, and they only published books they thought would make them a profit. The traditional publishing model is based on book sales—if people buy the book, the publisher makes money. Since their profits depend on selling a high volume of copies, they can only afford to publish books they believe will be successful."

"That's kind of like a Hollywood producer making a movie," Mark said. "They won't fund a film unless they think it'll be a blockbuster or at least make back its investment."

"Very true. They focus on what will appeal to a wide audience. Meanwhile, movies that are more independently-minded—artistic, niche, or message-driven—are often self-financed or produced by independent studios. The same is true for books. Not every author writes a book in order to sell thousands of copies, and that's okay. In fact, many of your books aren't necessarily about making huge sales—they're about building your businesses."

"That's true," Sarah said. "I was actually thinking of giving away many of my books at bridal shows to attract potential clients."

"Great idea! If even one person signs up for your services because of your book, that's a huge win for you. The revenue from that client would far exceed any profit you'd make from selling copies of the book."

"I guess the same is true for me. If I get one real estate listing from my book—and it's a million-dollar home—I'd make a significant commission."

"Precisely. So, in your case, it actually makes more sense to give books away to potential clients rather than focus on book sales. The profits from a signed contract are far greater than the few dollars you might make on a book sale.

"I'm not saying your book shouldn't be available for purchase," Amy added. "In fact, having your book listed on Amazon builds your credibility and can attract people outside of your existing network. But the real power of your books lies in how they support your business—whether you're handing them out at events, selling them at workshops, or simply displaying them in your office. It also helps to have your book available for sale in online bookstores."

"So now that you put it that way," Mark said, "does that mean we all have to self-publish? If our books won't sell enough to benefit a traditional publisher, why would they want us?"

"That's an excellent point," Amy said. "Nowadays, there are generally three different paths to publication.

"Traditional publishing is when a publisher covers all the costs of production and distribution. Because they bear the financial risk, they only accept books they believe will generate a strong return on investment. That's probably not the right path for most of us here.

"Self-publishing is when you do everything yourself. You're responsible for covering all the costs and decisions—editing, cover design, distribution, layout, whatever comes up—and you also manage the entire process.

"In hybrid publishing, both the author and the publisher share responsibilities. The publisher handles all the production work, while the author typically subsidizes the costs through fees. The advantage of hybrid publishing is that you end up with a professionally produced book without having to oversee every detail yourself. Plus, many hybrid publishers offer post-publication support, such as marketing and promotion."

"That sounds like exactly what I need," said Mark. "Someone to handle all the work for me."

"That may be true," Amy said. "But even if someone else is doing the work, I want to walk you through the process so you understand what's involved. That way, when you're evaluating publishers, you'll know what to look for. Not every publisher is the right fit for every book."

"So, what exactly are the steps we need to take?" Sharon asked. "I'm ready to make a list."

"Good for you!" Amy said. "After writing your manuscript, the next step is editing. There are several types of editing you will want."

"Is a computer program like Grammarly the same as an editor?" Mark asked.

"Grammarly is more like a proofreader. It catches mistakes and makes suggestions, but it doesn't get into the deeper aspects of your writing. It can be useful for sentence structure improvements, but you need to review its suggestions carefully. For example, Grammarly tends to overuse commas. If I accepted all of its suggestions, my writing wouldn't sound like me anymore."

"I see," Kami said. "So, what are the other types of editing?"

"The deepest level of editing is developmental editing. This focuses on the book as a whole—whether it answers the questions it sets out to answer. In fiction, developmental editing involves character development, believability, and emotional engagement. In nonfiction, it deals with structure, clarity, and voice—making sure the book speaks to the right audience."

"Well, that sounds like what we've already been working on with you," Aidan said.

"That's right. I've been working with you as a developmental editor and coach, helping to shape your books. But if someone were working alone, they might need to seek developmental editing at this stage. Another approach is using 'beta readers'—people who read your manuscript and give overall feedback. They're not looking for typos or missing commas, but rather, evaluating whether the book is engaging, informative, and enjoyable."

"My husband, Ryan, has been reading my manuscript," Sarah said, laughing. "All he says is, 'Why are you so obsessed with royalty?'"

Amy chuckled. "I'm glad he's reading it, but he's probably not your target audience."

"That's true. I also had my best friend read it, and she had a very different reaction."

"In general, beta readers should be members of your target audience," Amy said. "Otherwise, you'll get feedback that isn't particularly helpful. For example, I don't personally enjoy horror books, even though I've read and published them. So, if I were a beta reader for a horror book, I'd probably say, 'This is too scary!'—which isn't useful feedback."

"So if we've all had developmental editing and beta readers," Mark asked, "what's the next stage of editing?"

"The next stage is line editing. This involves going through your manuscript line by line, improving structure, clarity, and readability. Sometimes a line editor is also a proofreader, checking for misspelling and such. Even if your editor does more than one thing at once, it isn't a bad idea to have someone take another look at your manuscript, as another set of eyes is always helpful.

"And while there are AI programs that can assist with these levels of editing, it is always best to have an eagle-eyed human assisting the AI, as well as doing the final proofread. Proofreading is what many people think of as editing—checking spelling, punctuation, capitalization, and other surface items. It is extremely important but certainly not the only editing to be done to improve and polish a manuscript for publication.

"After editing, when you truly have the best, cleanest manuscript possible, it will need to be formatted. This is when book size, margins, headers and footers, font choices, chapter headings, and page layout all come into play. With a typical novel that simply includes text on a page, this list may not be much, but with books that include images, tables, infographics, or other features included in many non-fiction books, this list might be much more extensive."

"Could a book include handwriting—like if I wanted to include original works or writings of our program participants?" asked Alex.

"Absolutely! Visually interesting add-ins can certainly help to engage the reader and draw them in emotionally to your book. Even novels are utilizing more visual aspects, including dialogue as text messaging and other features."

"You mentioned infographics—I think it would be amazing to include some in my book. How do I create them?" asked Sam.

"I think that infographics are definitely going to be pivotal to your book, as it will help the reader to understand and visualize the issues you are discussing around the world. Canva is a great—and free—graphic design tool that allows you to create your own infographics. Once you've designed them, you can download them as image files and easily insert them into your book. I'm looking forward to seeing what you come up with."

"Maps, too?"

"Definitely include maps! I'm not sure most of us knew where Ethiopia was before meeting you!" Everyone laughed, though with a hint of embarrassment.

"Once you have your manuscript laid out the way you want, you will look at things like copyright designation, ISBN numbers—which is an individual number assigned to each book and format available—Library of Congress numbers, and distribution—which is making your book available to others publicly. Honestly, you would be best off looking at your options for distribution before committing to your layout and format, because different possibilities will have varying requirements. For example, self-publishing through Amazon—which they call KDP—may have different book sizes, margins, and cover requirements than self-publishing through something else, like Barnes and Noble or Draft2Digital. If you format first before deciding, be aware that you may need to make alterations to your layout."

"I can definitely understand why going with a publisher saves an awful lot of time and work," Kami said.

"It definitely can. Although some people like to be involved in every aspect of their book, others would prefer the heavy-lifting done by professionals. It is kind of like landscaping—

some people love to work in the garden and hand-select every flower and fruit they plant, while others don't even want to mow their own lawn. Neither is right nor wrong—just different strokes for different folks.

"And just as there is no one right way to publish your book, there is no one publisher that is right for all authors. I'm delighted to have worked with all of you over these past weeks and would be proud to continue working with you toward publication, if you choose. However, there are plenty of publishers and options available, and I would encourage all of you to prepare a query letter and send it along to publishers you may be interested in working with. A query letter includes much of the same information as we worked on in your book description, including a book overview or synopsis and comparison to similar books. You will also want to include your own bio, as it establishes why you are the right person to write this book. But, unlike your book description, you aren't trying to convince someone to buy your book. Rather, your goal is to entice the potential publishers to want to publish your book. You will want to describe your ideal reader, which is called your target market, and how you plan to reach that reader. A potential publisher is looking at your query letter to determine if you have a solid book idea, if you are qualified to write the book, and what kind of marketing you plan to do for your book. Remember, publishers want to select books that have the highest chance of succeeding, as they are essentially investing in you and your book for the future. Also, you should include your manuscript—or at least a sizable sample—along with your letter.

"Some potential publishers may require you to complete an application form. For others, you may send your query letter and manuscript or sample along to an email address. In either case, preparing your query letter will give you more options for applying to publishers and will also help you in filling out any publication applications you may find.

"Once you have applied, a response may take anywhere from days to months, depending on their own scheduling. And honestly, some publishers may never reply, so it is a good not to take things too personally regarding publication applications. Remember—not every publisher is the right fit for every author, nor is every book the right fit for every publisher.

"So let's chat a bit about the parts of a query letter that were not part of your book description—namely, your target market, your own credentials as an author, and your plans to market your book. Why don't we start with you, Kami?"

"Well, I'm a fairly new real estate agent, so I'm afraid I don't have any credentials."

"While you may feel that way, the fact is that you are a certified real estate agent—isn't that right? And also, since you have contributors in your book, your query letter should include their experience and credentials, as well. In fact, I'll bet once you add it all together, you probably have over 100 years of real estate experience among your group of collaborators."

"Well, that's true, and it certainly makes me feel better! And I suppose my target market is older adults looking to sell their homes. But what do I say about a marketing plan?"

"I know that you have already started posting on social media, so mentioning the platforms you are active on, along with the number of followers you have amassed thus far, is a great way to show that you are proactive even before publication. Plus, if you have any plans for featuring your contributors in workshops, talks, or other collaborations, be sure to mention that, as well."

"Thanks! I took notes, as I can't possibly remember all of that or come up with something to write right away."

"Of course, mull it over before writing your query letter. Also, I will email everyone a query letter template to remind you of that major 'questions asked' sections you will want to include. Mark, tell us about your target reader."

"I suppose divorced people who want to protect their assets are my target readers. And should I mention my financial certifications in my bio?"

"Absolutely! And if you have any licenses, have ever won any awards, or have any other notable achievements that would be worth mentioning, too. And what about your marketing plan?"

"I have a Facebook page and a LinkedIn account. That doesn't sound like much."

"True, but one reason writing a query letter is a good exercise —even if you plan to self-publish—is so you can think about marketing and make some plans. Regardless of your publication method, you will certainly want to think about your marketing plans. These can include social media, podcasts, workshops, talks, and other strategies to get the word out about you and your book. Sarah—tell us about your target market, author credentials and marketing plan."

"Hmmm ... is my target market brides planning a wedding or lovers of royalty? Or somehow both?"

"Good point! I would say one target would be women between 20 and 40 who love royalty. Some may be brides, some may be future brides, and most will know brides. But another target would be actual brides, so your marketing plan could include outreach to both brides and royal lovers."

"Unlike Kami and Mark, I don't have any certifications or licenses. So what would I say about me?"

"Even though wedding planners don't have any certifications, you can certainly mention your experience. And since your experience in terms of years in business is rather limited, instead it would be good to say something less numerical, perhaps something like coordinated weddings for brides with a variety of budgets and styles, from tasteful elopement ceremonies to full formal weddings and everything in between, or something like that."

"Wow! That certainly makes my limited experience sounds much more comprehensive."

"Exactly! And as for your marketing plan, you have certainly been active in both bridal groups online and royalty-lovers groups."

"And I even got a 'like' from the official account of Princess Catherine! I think that was my proudest moment, but is that something I would write in my bio?"

"Why not? It certainly shows that your social media reach is international, and that your accounts have even caught the attention of the Royal Family. That is most definitely something to mention!

"Aidan, what are your thoughts about your target market, author credentials and marketing strategy?"

"Well, I am a licensed electrician, and our company hires only licensed workers, but I kinda liked the way you described Sarah—talking about the range of work she has done."

"That could definitely work for you, too. Perhaps something like: 'From simple home repairs through full house renovations and restorations, Aidan has seen and worked with it all, whether it's new construction or a century-old home.' How does that sound to you?"

"Really nice. Heck, I'd hire me! That sounds like copy I should put on my website, too."

"Absolutely! You can see why I thought writing a query letter was a valuable lesson for us all, even for those who plan to self-publish. How about your target market?"

"I'm thinking that rather than ages or gender like Sarah, I would like to target homeowners. Is that OK?"

"Of course! And what are your thoughts about marketing?"

"Well, I was at Home Depot the other day and noticed that they sell books, so I guess that would be the dream—having my book sold at Home Depot."

"That's certainly a great goal but not necessarily a marketing plan. How you plan to share your book with others is your marketing plan. Most of you here have a local business, one where the location of your clients matters. For example, while Sarah's book might impact brides and wedding planning all around the country, she will want to take actual clients only in her local area. Isn't that right, Sarah?"

"That's true for my current business model, although I suppose there are wedding planners who meet virtually and do everything online, traveling to the wedding location just for the actual event. I guess for the right price that would be feasible."

"I can see that. Perhaps Kami is a better example of a local business, one where the customers must be from a specific area."

"That's true," agreed Kami. "While it would be fun for people to like my book all over the country, I could only really sell houses in my area. For one thing, I am only licensed in my state. But some agents I know, who are licensed in Florida also, can handle transactions in both states."

"Wow—I never thought about that! So Sarah, perhaps I shouldn't presume anything, but rather, ask you the question: where do you want your future customers to come from?"

"Well, you aren't wrong, Amy. It would certainly make my life much easier if my customers were within a relatively close location. So what does that mean to marketing?"

"As one of the benefits of writing a book to build your business is to increase your exposure and credibility, marketing it nationally can only help you overall. However, it is good to keep in mind that your book is also there to serve as a direct business driver, and so you will want to use it to actually get more business. Honestly, that could mean promoting it globally by using social media to build an audience online but also distributing your book locally, whether you are giving away copies at a local bridal showcase or directly to potential clients when they book a consultation."

"My business is a mix of in-person and online services," volunteered Tina. "There are couples I met with in-person while others might receive anything from one-on-one counseling to taking part in group workshops online, without ever leaving the comfort of their homes."

"Then definitely your target market is national. How would you describe a person in your target market?"

"I'm not really sure how I can target people in troubled relationships. Any thoughts?"

"Well, certainly by posting relationship tips and such, you would attract potential readers looking to improve their relationships. But as Aidan noted, the divorce rate is such that if you targeted people of a certain age-bracket, you'll probably stumble upon many couples in trouble. In general, who is more likely to contact you for counseling—men or women?"

"By far it's women who contact me, and I would say they're likely in their 40s or 50s. Wow—I never realized that I actually have a target market until now. That will be so helpful for my marketing overall. Thank you!"

"I knew that working on our query letters would pay off, but I didn't realize it would happen so quickly! I'll be sending you all a worksheet for publication to help you figure out what your best next step is toward publication."

THINK ABOUT ...

Think about your current publishing goals—do you dream of holding your book in hand quickly, reaching a wide audience, or maintaining full creative control? How does each publishing path support or limit these goals?

Do you know of other authors with positive—or negative—experiences in publishing their book? Research a few options (they could be publishing companies or even asking others about their experiences) and compare items like contacts, transparency, testimonials, and ownership to begin to discern the best fit for you and your book.

What does "success" mean to you in regards to your book—personal pride, increased income, wide-reaching impact, or something else? Has your definition changed over time? Write your "Author Success Statement" in 2-3 sentences, defining what will make you feel as if you have achieved your goal.

10
IT'S PARTY TIME!

Over the next several weeks, Sarah's book came together piece by piece. As she completed each section, she sent it over to Amy for a second set of eyes. After all the sections were complete, Amy's editor looked over everything for consistency and correctness. Sarah organized her book into chapters, added pictures, and, at Amy's suggestion, included a section on wedding planning at the end with leading questions and blank spaces for brides to fill in their favorites.

The cover designer brought Sarah's vision to life, and after sending a sample to a friend who matched their demographic for advice, they selected a final cover. Sarah and Amy started talking about a book release event, and Sarah's social media buzzed with excitement.

Sarah decided to turn the book event into a true business driver by creating a bridal showcase specifically for high-end vendors who worked with her ideal clients and vision. As the host of the event, not only would she have the opportunity to meet prospective clients and feature her new book, but she was also making connections with other vendors working at her ideal price point. These vendors saw her as an expert on royal-style weddings and were excited to be part of a bridal showcase that attracted the right clientele.

With Amy handling all the logistics of publishing and printing books, Sarah was free to make connections and order fun food and favors for the event, including tiaras for the brides, sample wedding cakes, and musicians fit for a queen's coronation. By the time the event rolled around, Sarah was already juggling both new clients in her target range and events on her calendar that would get her in front of even more people who shared her vision.

The day finally arrived, and Sarah was able to meet Amy for the very first time. Amy presented Sarah with a special quill pen, with Sarah's monogram engraved on it, for her to sign books.

"I feel like a queen myself!" Sarah exclaimed excitedly. "I can't believe I'm actually here, not only holding a book with my name across the cover but also running the business of my dreams. I have weddings lined up that I am truly excited about—ones that, if I weren't the wedding planner, I would hope to be a guest at. You truly made my dreams come true."

"I am so glad to see you happy, Sarah," Amy said. "But it was you who had a vision and worked to see it through. When we first met, you asked if it was going to be hard and if I thought you'd be able to do it. What are your thoughts now? Was this harder than you expected? Was it more stressful, or would you recommend it to someone else?"

Sarah quickly replied, "Several months ago, when I was sitting with Michelle at a business meeting, talking about the book she had written, I thought it sounded absolutely overwhelming. She talked about how easy you made it and how repurposing all the content from the book into social media feeds helped build her business on several levels. She also said that working on the book gave her a much clearer business vision and helped her streamline her target market and message to focus solely on her mission.

"Now that we have reached the finish line with this book, I couldn't agree with her more. Yes, it certainly added tasks to my to-do list, but the investment in time paid off in spades. Targeting exactly what type of business I wanted to run and what type of clients I wanted to work with, so that the book would be right on message, was invaluable to me and helped me see where I had been missing the mark in my business previously.

"And certainly, the research and writing took time, but using that same material for promoting on social media really energized my feeds and gave me direction. I had no idea what I was supposed to be writing, to be honest. Unless I was promoting a specific event, I felt like I was hitting a brick wall every time I should be posting. Now I have actual direction online, and I'm attracting exactly the right kind of followers. People both in my industry, as well as newly engaged brides-to-be, view me as the expert on royal weddings, and I'm getting referrals to new clients who want to realize that exact vision.

"Not to mention, it was an awful lot of fun writing this book, and I couldn't be more excited to be sitting here, signing copies for new readers. Amy, working on this book has completely transformed my business, and I would definitely tell others that while there was certainly work involved, it was fun work that will help them not just with their book, but with their business, and will truly change the course of their business life. I couldn't be happier."

"I love how you planned a big event and included your referral partners in your book launch. That's such a great idea that other authors in our group could use, as well."

"Yes, I can definitely picture Kami coordinating a real estate showcase for her book release and inviting all the contributors from her book. What an outstanding event to attract people interested in buying, selling, or simply learning about real estate!"

"Exactly! And Sharon is so excited about her new book and topic that we were just talking about her doing a series of events at wineries and liquor stores. She wants to combine a wine tasting with a talk on the chemistry behind wine production and sell her books alongside the venue selling wine. She's already reached out to a few locations, and they can't wait for her book to be finished so they can book an event. Plus, each location will sell her book afterward as part of their product line."

"Wow—book events plus ongoing sales, even when she isn't there. You can't get much better than that!"

"A national conference for financial planners invited Mark as a guest panelist, and he plans to debut his book there. He'll have a vendor table with books, flyers, and a QR code offering a free book sample to collect contact information."

"That sounds like a great way to debut his book—with a national audience!"

"Aidan is still finishing his book. I think he wants every 'i' dotted and 't' crossed before discussing the next steps.

Knowing his line of work, that doesn't surprise me one bit! And Tina is thrilled about her upcoming workshop series and retreat for married couples who want to improve their communication. She's still writing, but I suspect she won't finish until after the retreat she's planning."

"That couples' retreat sounds amazing—working on your marriage in beautiful Tuscany! It almost makes me wish my marriage was in trouble!"

"Apparently, many are, because she's sold out and even had to offer a second retreat! Although her book is unfinished, sharing online excerpts has greatly expanded her audience."

"That's great. I'm sure she wants her book completed, but it's wonderful that even working on it has boosted her business."

"Absolutely! It's helped so much that she barely has time to finish writing—a real catch-22!"

"I so miss meeting with our group regularly. I'm glad that we're all connected on social media so that I can see what everyone is up to and cheer along from afar!"

"I miss our meetings, as well, but it seems the group is too busy enjoying the rewards of their hard work to have time for one anyway," Amy laughed. "By the way, I don't know if you heard the news that Sam was accepted at the London School of Economics. While we'll never know if writing the book on global environmental issues positively impacted the admissions committee, it certainly didn't hurt. Plus Sam got so excited by the additional research to fill out the book content that I wouldn't be surprised if there weren't more environmental impact papers and books to come."

"That is fantastic news! Has Alex launched the non-profit yet?"

"Not yet. Working on the book actually raised more questions than it answered, leading Alex to restructure the non-profit to focus on areas more likely to attract grants and donations. It also clarified where the funding would likely come from. Instead of rushing to publish and risk targeting the wrong audience, Alex decided to wait until key goals are met to better position the book. Similar to Sharon's shift in direction, Alex realized the original concept didn't quite fit the intended audience and is now ensuring the non-profit is set up for success by appealing to those most likely to support arts education for children. When it comes to rethinking a book before publication, it is always better late than never!"

"And when it does open, I plan to be at the opening, as I live just a few towns away."

"That would be amazing if you went. But first we have your very exciting book launch to attend to—not to mention your growing business."

"You said it—I finally have people calling me instead of the other way around, and they're brides with wedding plans that excite me. I *am* the luckiest bridal planner ever!

THINK ABOUT ...

What kind of book launch event reflects your personality, brand, and audience? Think about events you've attended or seen online—what stood out? Would you prefer something intimate and cozy, big and bold, virtual, in-person, or a mix?

How can you use your launch party to build excitement and create lasting connections with readers and supporters? Plan out a simple *launch content checklist*—before, during, and after the event. For example:

- Before: behind-the-scenes prep video
- During: photos with guests holding the book
- After: thank-you post with highlights or testimonials

Who can you invite or partner with to help make your book launch a bigger success? Do you have local businesses, creative friends, influencers, or fellow authors who could support your event? What kind of collaborations would be fun and mutually beneficial?

PART TWO
TAKE ACTION

Are You Ready to Turn Your Expertise Into a Book—and Your Business Into a Brand?

If you saw yourself in Sarah's story, you're not alone. In Part 2 of *Bookology*, you'll move from inspiration to action. Through guided worksheets, prompts, and strategic exercises, you'll uncover your unique message, define your ideal audience, and create a clear roadmap to write and publish a book that elevates your business, attracts dream clients, and positions you as the expert you already are.

No fluff. No guesswork. Just the step-by-step tools you need to write your book—and rewrite your future.

1
WHY WRITE A BOOK

Publishing a book is one of the most powerful ways to elevate your business and refine your professional focus. It allows you to position yourself as an expert in your field, attract the types of clients you most want to work with, and carve out a niche that reflects your values and aspirations.

Perhaps, like Sarah, you initially entered your business as a "jack of all trades," saying yes to any opportunity that came your way. While this approach may have been necessary to establish yourself in the early days, it can leave you feeling stretched thin, frustrated, and unfulfilled. Writing a book offers a chance to recalibrate—to tell your story, define your expertise, and attract the clients and projects that align with your passions and strengths.

To reconnect with your core purpose and shape your book's message, start by reflecting on your business journey.

REFLECT ON THE BEGINNING

Revisiting the reasons you started your business can offer clarity and inspiration:

- **Why did you start your business?**

What excited you about this path? What vision drove you forward?

- **Who were your ideal clients when you started?**

What kinds of people or organizations did you dream of serving?

- **What type of work or projects inspired you most?**

Were there particular services or creative pursuits you couldn't wait to tackle?

EVALUATE YOUR GROWTH AND CURRENT FOCUS

Over time, your experiences have likely shaped your perspective. Use this growth to refine your professional priorities:

- **What types of clients do you prefer working with now?**

Consider the qualities of clients who energize you and make your work enjoyable.

- **Are there clients or projects you've taken on that you'd prefer to avoid in the future?**

Identify patterns that consistently drain your time, energy, or resources.

- **What kinds of projects bring you joy and fulfillment?**

Pinpoint the work that feels most meaningful and rewarding.

- **What projects generate the highest revenue for your business?**

Align your focus with opportunities that provide both financial and personal rewards.

- **Are there tasks that require more time and effort than they're worth?**

These areas might be better delegated, outsourced, or eliminated entirely.

FOCUS ON YOUR FUTURE

As you evaluate your current situation, think about how writing a book can help you focus your business and attract the clients and projects that matter most. Answer these reflective prompts honestly to gain clarity:

1. Am I spending my time each day doing what I want?

    Strongly Agree ... Strongly Disagree ... Sometimes but not always

2. Am I able to handpick clients who fit my ideal customer profile?

    Strongly Agree ... Strongly Disagree ... Sometimes but not always

3. Do I feel valued for the work I'm doing?

    Strongly Agree ... Strongly Disagree ... Sometimes but not always

4. Does my work align with my long-term goals and vision?

    Strongly Agree ... Strongly Disagree ... Sometimes but not always

5. Am I building a reputation in the areas I want to specialize in?

    Strongly Agree ... Strongly Disagree ... Sometimes but not always

6. Do I feel inspired and motivated by my current projects?

    Strongly Agree ... Strongly Disagree ... Sometimes but not always

7. Am I leveraging my unique skills and expertise to their fullest potential?

    Strongly Agree ... Strongly Disagree ... Sometimes but not always

8. Do I feel financially secure and satisfied with the revenue my business generates?

    Strongly Agree ... Strongly Disagree ... Sometimes but not always

9. Am I consistently attracting opportunities that excite me?

    Strongly Agree ... Strongly Disagree ... Sometimes but not always

10. Do I have the flexibility in my schedule to pursue creative or strategic projects?

    Strongly Agree ... Strongly Disagree ... Sometimes but not always

11. Is my current workload sustainable and balanced with my personal life?

    Strongly Agree ... Strongly Disagree ... Sometimes but not always

12. Am I effectively communicating my value to my clients and audience?

>Strongly Agree ... Strongly Disagree ... Sometimes but not always

13. Do I feel confident in the direction my business is heading?

>Strongly Agree ... Strongly Disagree ... Sometimes but not always

HOW WRITING A BOOK FITS IN

A book can be a strategic tool to realign your business with your goals. It lets you:

- Showcase your unique expertise and insights.
- Speak directly to your ideal clients, helping them understand the value you offer.
- Filter out mismatched opportunities by clearly defining your niche.

Your book becomes more than a marketing tool—it's a way to clarify your vision, reconnect with your purpose, and create a business that serves both you and your clients better.

2

HOW YOUR BOOK WILL TRANSFORM YOUR BUSINESS

There is no doubt about it—having a book "to your name" sets you apart like nothing else can. In fact, once you've written a book, it becomes an integral part of your professional identity. The words "author of _____" will often appear right after your name, even before other credentials. It's a badge of honor that instantly signals expertise, authority, and credibility.

How would adding "author of _____" to your bio impact your career or business?

- Would it open doors to new opportunities such as speaking engagements, interviews, collaborations, or client acquisitions?
- Would being "the author" in your field make you stand out in a crowded market?

Think about the industries or circles you move in. Perhaps you've noticed that everyone from news reporters to Oprah gravitates toward authors when seeking an "expert" opinion.

Why? Because authors are presumed to have deeper insights and specialized knowledge. If an article writer or news producer had to choose between two similar professionals to quote or feature, what criteria would help them decide? Most likely, the one who has written a book. *"They must know something—they wrote a book!"* is the default assumption.

REFLECTIVE PROMPTS TO CONSIDER

1. What do you want your book to say about you and your expertise?

- Is it solving a problem for your audience?
- Is it sharing your unique journey, methods, or perspective?

2. How can a book support your professional goals?

- Could it help you secure speaking engagements, media appearances, or new clients?
- Would it provide you with a clear and polished way to share your story or business philosophy?

3. What opportunities are currently closed to you that having a book might unlock?

- Do you long to be a podcast guest, spreading your message to others?
- Could a book help you expand your network or cross into new markets?

4. How would having a book improve your confidence and positioning in your industry?

- Would you feel more prepared to call yourself an expert in your field?
- Could it enhance your ability to negotiate fees, command respect, or attract high-quality opportunities?

THE NECESSITY OF A BOOK FOR SPEAKERS

Would more speaking engagements boost your business or credibility? Whether you want to speak professionally or simply to attract more clients, a book is a game-changer. Take a look at any speaker application form—from school workshops to national keynote stages—and you'll find a field asking for the title of your book. In many cases, it's not just an option—it's a requirement.

Audiences and event organizers want to hear from *"experts,"* and nothing establishes your expertise quite like being a published author. Imagine how your introduction would sound at a conference:

> "Today's speaker is Sarah Jones, author of *Elegant Events: Mastering the Art of Wedding Planning*."

Now think of the alternative:

> "Today's speaker is Sarah Jones, a wedding planner."

Which one carries more weight and sets a tone of authority?

A BOOK AS A PROFESSIONAL ASSET

Beyond speaking engagements, consider how a book can serve as a versatile tool:

- Sales Tool: Use it to attract and secure clients.
- Business Card Upgrade: Hand a book to a potential client instead of a brochure—it's a powerful differentiator.
- Legacy Builder: Establish yourself as a leader in your field, leaving a lasting impact.
- Networking Magnet: Open doors to collaborations, partnerships, and high-profile connections.

EXAMPLES OF SUCCESS THROUGH AUTHORSHIP

- A financial planner used their book to simplify investment concepts, helping them land speaking gigs and gain high-value clients.
- A fitness trainer published a book on sustainable fitness, which not only boosted their credibility but also launched an online coaching program.
- A professor authored a book to support their research and teaching, gaining tenure and invitations to contribute to major academic conferences.
- A small business owner wrote about their entrepreneurial journey, attracting media attention and new partnerships that expanded their reach.

FINAL THOUGHTS

Would you benefit from these opportunities? Writing a book is not just about the final product—it's about the journey of clarifying your ideas, defining your ideal audience, and honing your message. It's a process that can strengthen your business or career long before the book is even published.

And always remember what E.B. White so wisely observed:

"Most people believe almost anything they see in print."

3
ESTABLISHING YOUR GOALS

There are countless reasons to write a book—just as there are countless types of authors. Finding your *why*—your core motivation for writing a book—is crucial to your success. Your *why* serves as your guiding light, helping you plan your content, prioritize your efforts, and persevere through the challenges until you write the final word. Whether your book serves as a professional milestone, a passion project, or a strategic tool, clarifying your purpose will keep you focused and motivated throughout the journey.

To help define your goals, reflect on the following statements and consider how they align with your vision. Check off the ones that resonate most with you, knowing it's perfectly fine to have more than one reason for writing your book.

Professional Branding:

Do you want to add "author of _____" to your bio to enhance your personal or professional brand?

Yes   No   Unsure

Industry Expertise:

Is establishing yourself as an expert in your field one of your primary reasons for writing a book?

Yes   No   Unsure

Client Attraction:

Do you want your book to act as a marketing tool that helps attract new clients or customers?

Yes   No   Unsure

Networking:

Do you see your book as a conversation starter or "ultimate business card" for building relationships with potential clients, partners, or collaborators?

Yes   No   Unsure

Teaching or Coaching:

Will your book be used as part of workshops, training sessions, or one-on-one coaching that you offer?

Yes   No   Unsure

Revenue Generation:

Do you want to sell your book at seminars, conferences, or online as an additional income stream?

Yes   No   Unsure

Audience Engagement:

Do you want your book to help you stay memorable and connected with event attendees after presentations or speeches?

Yes   No   Unsure

Reputation Building:

Is improving your credibility and reputation within your industry an important goal for you?

Yes   No   Unsure

Storytelling:

Is sharing your personal journey, experiences, or lessons learned one of your motivations for writing a book?

Yes   No   Unsure

Legacy:

Do you want your book to serve as a legacy project, documenting your knowledge or story for future generations?

Yes   No   Unsure

Inspirational Impact:

Are you driven by the desire to inspire or motivate others with your insights or experiences?

Yes   No   Unsure

Creative Expression:

Do you see writing a book as a way to express yourself creatively or to explore your thoughts and ideas in-depth?

Yes   No   Unsure

SCORING AND REFLECTION

After answering the questions, identify which responses were a firm "Yes." Group similar goals together (e.g., branding, teaching, inspiration) to determine which areas matter most to you. This will help you prioritize your focus as you plan and write your book. If many answers are "Unsure," spend time reflecting on what success looks like for you and your book.

EXPLORING YOUR GOALS

#1. Establishing Professional Authority

I want to promote and further my business or career by adding "author of _____" to my bio.

> Becoming an author automatically elevates your professional profile. When people see "author" alongside your name, they associate you with credibility, expertise, and authority in your field. This recognition can help you stand out in competitive industries where establishing your personal brand is essential. Writing a book allows you to define your narrative, share your unique perspective, and showcase your qualifications in a way that resonates with potential clients, partners, and industry leaders.
>
> For example, professionals in consulting, coaching, or leadership roles often find that writing a book helps them build

trust with their audience. Your book becomes more than just a credential; it's a door-opener for opportunities like keynote speaking engagements, collaborations with influencers, or invitations to exclusive industry events. Additionally, having a book to your name can make it easier to negotiate higher fees or positions, as it demonstrates your thought leadership and depth of knowledge.

#2. Positioning Yourself as an Expert

I would like to establish myself as relevant and an "expert" in my field by writing a book on a particular topic.

In today's fast-paced and crowded marketplace, being recognized as an expert is a significant advantage. Writing a book allows you to present a deep dive into your area of expertise, demonstrating your authority and mastery of the subject. A well-written book positions you as someone who not only understands the field but also has the ability to teach, influence, and inspire others within it.

For instance, if you're a financial advisor, writing a book about strategies for wealth management could help you attract clients who are seeking someone knowledgeable and trustworthy. Similarly, if you're in the tech industry, a book about emerging trends or innovative solutions could make you a go-to thought leader in your niche. Experts are often the ones invited to take part in media interviews, write for respected publications, or lead panels at industry events—and your book can serve as the foundation for all these opportunities.

#3. Using Your Book as a Marketing Tool

A book would act as the ultimate "business card" to distribute to prospective clients and referral sources.

A book is not just a marketing tool—it's a conversation starter, a relationship builder, and a trust accelerator. Unlike a traditional business card, which can easily be overlooked or discarded, a book is tangible and lasting. It conveys a level of seriousness and professionalism that sets you apart from competitors. By sharing your insights, success stories, or proven methods, your book builds rapport with potential clients before you even meet them.

Think about the impact of handing someone a signed copy of your book. It creates a sense of personal connection and value that a brochure or flyer never could. Your book might include calls to action, such as links to your website, contact information, or invitations to follow you on social media. This transforms your book into a dynamic tool that not only markets your services but also leads readers toward taking the next step in working with you.

#4. Integrating Your Book into Workshops or Training

I would like to use my book in workshops or training sessions —either as a workbook for one-on-one coaching or as a resource for group presentations.

If you lead workshops, training sessions, or coaching programs, your book can serve as an invaluable resource. Designing your book as a companion to your teaching allows you to reinforce the concepts you're sharing, provide actionable exercises, and ensure participants retain the knowledge they've gained. Whether it's a detailed guide, a workbook with space for reflection and practice, or a resource manual, your book becomes an integral part of your educational process.

For example, life coaches might create books with journaling prompts and strategies tailored to their clients' goals. Corporate trainers could write books that summarize key frameworks or methodologies used in their sessions. This not only enhances the learning experience for participants but also positions you as a leader in your niche. Attendees are more likely to recommend you to others or engage with your services when they feel they've received lasting value from both your teachings and your book.

#5. Boosting Visibility Through Sales and Distribution

I would like to sell my book at seminars, conferences, and speaking engagements to remain memorable.

One of the challenges many professionals face is remaining memorable after delivering a speech or presentation. Attendees may enjoy your talk but forget the finer details as the days pass. Your book serves as a tangible reminder of your message, your expertise, and your personal brand.

Selling or distributing your book at events provides participants with an opportunity to continue engaging with your content long after the seminar ends. As they read your book, they'll revisit the key takeaways from your talk and develop a deeper appreciation for your insights. This extended engagement can lead to new opportunities, such as future bookings, referrals, or consulting projects.

Additionally, your book can help spread your influence beyond the room. Attendees may share it with friends, colleagues, or supervisors, broadening your reach to potential clients or collaborators. Some professionals even find that their books generate additional revenue streams through bulk sales to organizations that incorporate them into their training or onboarding programs.

Other Goals to Consider

Don't feel confined by these examples. Perhaps you want to use your book as a legacy project, documenting your journey or experiences to inspire others. Or maybe it's a way to share your philosophy, processes, or innovative solutions with a wider audience. Whatever your goals, knowing your purpose will shape every decision you make, from the structure of your content to the marketing strategy you employ.

Take a moment to write down additional reasons that are uniquely yours. By identifying your "why," you'll not only find clarity in your purpose but also build the momentum you need to see your book through to completion.

_____

_____

_____

_____

4
EIGHT TYPES OF BOOKS

You don't need to reinvent the wheel when writing a book, as there are many different structures you can adopt for your own book, each with a different level of time commitment, creativity, and personal writing requirements. Take a look at the following and see which book type most appeals to you.

BOOK TYPE #1—BOOK OF IDEAS/TIPS

Books structured as lists of tips, ideas, or principles are straightforward to write and highly appealing to readers. They offer quick, actionable insights, positioning you as an approachable expert in your field. These books are concise, easy to navigate, and perfect for readers who want immediate, tangible takeaways.

Examples:

- *50 Great Myths of Popular Psychology*
- *25 Biblical Laws of Success*

- *17 Indisputable Laws of Teamwork*

Potential Title Ideas:

- *10 Wedding Hacks for a Stress-Free Big Day*
- *25 Secrets to Building a Thriving Business*
- *101 Ways to Save Money Without Sacrificing Style*

If you go to Amazon and simply type "50 ways to _____," you will hit upon a jackpot of book titles. Whether you go with 50 or 5, books set up in this manner are a breeze to write, set you up as an approachable "expert" in your field, and are enticing to read, as the reader feels as if they are going to glean tangible, applicable tips in a hurry. Brainstorm below on some "tips" titles you might use for your book.

_____

_____

_____

BOOK TYPE #2—BOOK OF QUESTIONS

Books of questions guide readers through self-reflection or decision-making processes. They also provide interactive value, as readers can write down their thoughts or answers directly in the book. These books are particularly effective for fields like personal development, finance, or business strategy.

Examples:

- *100 Questions Every First-Time Home Buyer Should Ask*
- *101 Questions to Ask Before You Get Engaged*

- *Life Organizer: The Essential Record Keeper and Estate Planner*

Potential Title Ideas:

- *50 Questions to Ask Before Hiring a Wedding Planner*
- *100 Questions to Shape Your Business Vision*
- *The Personal Growth Workbook: Questions for a Better You*

Whether you're in finance or personal growth, you surely ask your clients a lot of questions—in some fields, the questions sum up a majority of what you do! And whether your questions are designed to lead your readers to further introspection or simply to record information, your primary goal of leading readers to YOU and the positives of working with you will be realized. A book of questions contains a lot of blank spaces—as you see below—and can be written easily. Think about some questions you can ask a potential client/customer, or perhaps collections of questions and record your thoughts and potential titles below.

_____

_____

_____

BOOK TYPE #3—CASE STUDIES/STORIES

Books filled with real-life stories or case studies are engaging and relatable. They provide readers with practical lessons and insights through narratives, making abstract concepts easier to understand. These stories can come from your own experiences, client successes, or even interviews with others.

Examples:

- *Case Studies in Abnormal Psychology*
- *12 Classic Tales from the World of Wall Street*
- *Real Estate Stories: Hilarious and Uncensored Tales From a Property Management Expert*

Potential Title Ideas:

- *Wedding Nightmares: True Tales and Lessons from the Aisle*
- *Client Success Stories: How Small Businesses Thrived Against the Odds*
- *The Creative Entrepreneur: Stories of Resilience and Innovation*

Books of stories are big hits with readers, and they love to read about others facing the same issues and challenges as themselves, yet coming out on top. As a writer, you can either draw upon your own experiences and stories—changing names and identifying information where appropriate—or research biographies or cases related to your target area. What are some stories you may wish to include in a book? Are there enough—from your own experiences or from other sources—to fill a book?

_____

_____

_____

BOOK TYPE #4— COMPILATIONS/COLLABORATIONS

Compilation books bring together multiple contributors, allowing you to feature a range of expertise without writing the entire book yourself. By inviting others to collaborate, you create a win-win situation where contributors gain exposure, and you benefit from their insights and networks.

Examples:

- *Insider Secrets for Small-to-Medium Business Owners by Top Business and Marketing Experts*
- *The Real Book of Real Estate: Real Experts. Real Stories. Real Life.*
- *Shared Wisdom: Tips from Business Experts on How You Can Achieve Success*

Potential Title Ideas:

- *The Wedding Planner's Guide: Advice from Industry Experts*
- *Voices of Success: Lessons from Today's Top Entrepreneurs*
- *The Business Builder's Playbook: Tips from Industry Leaders*

When in doubt, have other people write your book for you! Not only can a compilation relieve you of the major portion of writing responsibilities, but inviting colleagues to partner in your project is a win-win for everyone. You end up with a book, they get exposure, and you gain incredible opportunities to network with others and give them a great opportunity—one which may be repaid to you in the future! Think about some possible subject areas—or even contributors—in the space below to ponder whether a compilation-style book is a good fit for you.

_____

_____

_____

BOOK TYPE #5—HOW-TO BOOK

How-to books provide step-by-step instructions on solving a problem or achieving a goal. These books are perfect for showcasing your expertise while offering practical help to readers. Instead of driving customers away, these books often convince readers they need your services.

Examples:

- *How to Win Friends and Influence People*
- *How to Pay Off Your Mortgage in 5 Years*
- *How to Read Literature Like a Professor*

Potential Title Ideas:

- *How to Plan the Perfect Wedding Without Losing Your Mind*
- *How to Market Your Small Business on a Shoestring Budget*
- *How to Create a Thriving Career Doing What You Love*

"How-to" books are such a popular topic area, they even have their own category on Amazon! Some authors worry that writing a how-to book will make people want to "do it themselves" and not enlist your services, but on the contrary, a how-to book exhibits your expertise in a particular area. Let's face it—some people like to do things themselves (even things they perhaps shouldn't be doing!), but others like to know a bit of information—just enough to realize that they are in way over their head! What are some things in your field that you could illuminate in a how-to book?

_____

_____

_____

BOOK TYPE #6—BUSINESS ALLEGORY

Business allegories use storytelling to convey lessons or principles in an engaging and relatable way. These books often feature fictional characters navigating challenges, making them more entertaining while still offering valuable insights.

Examples:

- *The Go-Giver: A Little Story About a Powerful Business Idea*
- *Who Moved My Cheese?*
- *The Five Dysfunctions of a Team*

Potential Title Ideas:

- *The Wedding Planner's Journey: Finding Success and Clients Through Storytelling*
- *The Entrepreneur's Roadmap: A Tale of Business Growth and Resilience*
- *The Creative's Path: Lessons from a Fictional Designer*

A business allegory is a book like this one you are reading, where the lessons are imparted through a narrative story so that the reader is caught up in the characters and their journey, and may be more receptive to a message than if it were spelled out for them. If you were to write a business allegory, what type of character would be the "star" of your book? And what challenges would they face?

_____

_____

_____

BOOK TYPE #7—TRANSFORMATIONAL MEMOIR

Transformational memoirs blend personal storytelling with inspiration and life lessons. These books highlight pivotal moments or challenges in the author's life that led to personal or professional growth. They are particularly effective for building trust and emotional connections with readers.

Examples:

- *Eat, Pray, Love*
- *The Glass Castle*
- *Becoming*

Potential Title Ideas:

- *From Bridezilla to Boss: How I Built My Wedding Planning Empire*
- *Turning Passion Into Profit: My Journey as a Small Business Owner*
- *Failing Forward: Lessons From My Journey to Success*

A transformation memoir is YOUR story—whether you overcame adversity as a child, had your business go bankrupt and brought it back from the ashes, or survived—and thrived—after a messy divorce. What challenges in your life could be the basis of a transformational memoir—and if not a whole book, perhaps the preface or introduction of your book?

_____

_____

_____

BOOK TYPE #8—A CHILDREN'S BOOK

Children's books that promote your business blend storytelling, education, and subtle branding to create an engaging experience for young readers—and their parents. These books often feature fun characters, age-appropriate lessons, and a narrative tied to your profession or industry.

Examples:

- *The Berenstain Bears Visit the Dentist*
- *The LEGO Ideas Book: Unlock Your Imagination*
- *Let's Meet a Construction Worker*

Potential Title Ideas:

- *Captain Kale and the Healthy Heroes* (for a health coach or nutritionist)
- *Milo Builds a Dream Business* (for an entrepreneur or business coach)
- *Luna's Magical Money Jar* (for a financial advisor)

Whether you're a dentist, real estate agent, coach, or chef, a well-crafted children's book can position you as a trusted expert, boost brand visibility, and even create a new revenue stream, and can be especially effective for businesses that serve families or want to build long-term community relationships. Would your business benefit from a children's book? Brainstorm about potential characters and themes below.

_____

_____

_____

5
YOUR WRITING STYLE AND METHODS

PLOTTER VS. PANTSER: WHICH ONE ARE YOU?

Writers tend to fall into two broad categories: Plotters and Pantsers. A plotter meticulously plans their book before writing, creating detailed outlines, structured chapters, and well-organized research. They thrive on logic, clarity, and efficiency, ensuring that each section follows a clear progression. Plotters often rely on tools like mind maps, spreadsheets, and detailed notes to maintain focus and cohesion. In contrast, a pantser (derived from "writing by the seat of their pants") takes a more spontaneous approach, diving into the writing process without a rigid structure. Pantsers let ideas flow freely, discovering connections and refining their book's direction as they write. While they may revisit organization later in the editing phase, they prefer to let creativity and intuition guide the first draft. Both approaches have their strengths—plotters benefit from clarity and efficiency, while pantsers embrace flexibility and discovery. Many nonfiction writers find a balance between the two, using a loose framework while allowing room for creative exploration.

ARE YOU A PLOTTER OR A PANTSER? A QUIZ FOR ASPIRING NONFICTION WRITERS

For each question, choose the answer that best reflects your natural style when approaching tasks, projects, or communication.

1. Before writing a long email, blog post, or letter, you:

    a) Jot down an outline or key points first.
    b) Dive in and let the message shape itself as you write.

2. When researching a topic (for work, school, or a personal project), you:

    a) Organize your findings into categories or notes
    b) Collect as you go and revisit things as needed

3. If you had to create a step-by-step guide or explain how to do something, you would:

    a) Plan each step ahead of time in a clear order
    b) Write the steps as they come to you, then reorganize them later

4. If you encountered a block while writing or working on a project, you'd likely:

    a) Revisit your outline or plan and move to a different part

b) Free-write, talk it out, or brainstorm until the next step comes to you

5. If you were preparing a speech or presentation, you'd most likely:

　　a) Write out a full script or detailed outline
　　b) Jot down key points and speak more spontaneously

6. When starting a project or paper, you prefer to:

　　a) Begin with an introduction or clear mission statement
　　b) Start with the body and write the intro once you know where it's going

7. When it comes to editing your work (even short pieces), you typically:

　　a) Edit and refine as you go
　　b) Draft everything first, then go back and revise heavily

8. When working on any kind of writing or creative project, you tend to:

　　a) Stick closely to a plan or checklist
　　b) Let your ideas evolve and follow them wherever they lead

9. In terms of planning your time, you are more likely to:

　　a) Set clear goals, timelines, or milestones

b) Work when inspiration strikes and adjust plans as needed

10. If a new idea pops into your head while working on a project, you:

a) Think about whether it fits with your current plan before using it
b) Run with it and adjust the rest of the plan later if needed

11. Do you tend to use tools to keep yourself organized (apps, spreadsheets, planners)?

a) Yes—I like to keep everything structured and in one place
b) Not really—I use whatever is convenient at the time

12. How do you imagine your book-writing process feeling?

a) Satisfying—following a well-thought-out plan and seeing it come to life
b) Surprising—discovering new directions as you write

RESULTS:

◆ **Mostly A's – You're a Plotter!**

You thrive on structure, planning, and clarity. Whether writing a book, planning a trip, or organizing your day, you like to know where you're headed before you begin. As a nonfiction writer, this means you'll likely benefit from:

- Creating a detailed outline before writing
- Mapping out chapters in advance
- Setting writing goals and timelines

Plotters often finish strong because they've thought through the whole journey. Just don't forget to leave a little space for spontaneity—sometimes your best ideas appear when you least expect them.

◆ Mostly B's – You're a Pantser!

You prefer to dive in and discover things along the way. Planning can feel restrictive to you—you're energized by momentum and creativity. When writing your book, you might:

- Start with a blank page and let your thoughts flow freely
- Discover your message and structure as you write
- Embrace revision as a key part of shaping your final product

Pantser energy is passionate and authentic—but be mindful not to lose your way mid-book. A light outline or writing buddy might help keep you grounded.

◆ A Mix of A's and B's – You're a Hybrid/ a 'Plantser!'

You like a bit of both worlds. You might start with a rough outline, but stay open to new directions. You may not need a fully developed roadmap—but you don't want to fly blind either.

As a nonfiction writer, your sweet spot could be:

- A flexible chapter outline that evolves as you write
- Writing in short sprints with occasional check-ins to stay aligned
- Balancing planning tools with creative freedom

Plantser writers often write books that are both well-structured and creatively rich—so embrace the balance!

FIND YOUR PERFECT WRITING TOOL!

There are countless ways to write, from typing at a computer to jotting down ideas on a napkin at a café. Some writers stick to one method, while others switch between tools depending on the task. Take this fun quiz to discover your writing preferences!

WHAT WRITING TOOL FITS YOUR TASK?

1. You need to make a grocery list. What do you use?

   a) A sticky note on the fridge
   b) The notes app on your phone
   c) A voice memo so you don't forget
   d) An index card in your pocket

2. You're brainstorming ideas for a new business. How do you get started?

   a) Sketch ideas in a notebook or on a whiteboard
   b) Open a document or spreadsheet
   c) Record your thoughts out loud

d) Use sticky notes or index cards to move things around

3. You have an amazing book idea and don't want to forget it. What's your go-to method?

   a) Jot it down in your notebook
   b) Type it into a digital notes app
   c) Record a voice memo for later use
   d) Scribble it on an index card for later

4. You're outlining a big speech or presentation. How do you organize your thoughts?

   a) Write out an outline in a journal
   b) Use presentation or word processing software
   c) Dictate key points into a voice-to-text app
   d) Arrange index cards with each talking point

5. You're drafting a heartfelt letter or personal journal entry. What do you reach for?

   a) A beautiful leather-bound journal
   b) Your laptop or tablet
   c) Your phone's dictation app - you feel more authentic speaking your thoughts
   d) A stack of index cards for each thought or memory

6. You're writing a detailed trip itinerary. What's your method?

   a) A travel notebook or planner
   b) A Google Doc or itinerary app
   c) Record your plans as spoken notes

d) Organize stops and notes on moveable cards

7. You need to create a to-do list for the week. How do you prefer to do it?

   a) A bullet journal with neat checkboxes
   b) A digital to-do list app
   c) Record your list as a voice note
   d) Sticky notes all over your desk

8. You're writing an important email but want to draft it first. Where do you do that?

   a) Write it in a notebook first to organize your thoughts
   b) Type it directly into the email draft
   c) Dictate it and edit the text later
   d) Scribble notes on paper before typing it out

9. You're working on a big creative project. How do you keep track of your ideas?

   a) A dedicated journal for inspiration
   b) A folder of digital notes and documents
   c) Voice recordings or dictated thoughts
   d) Index cards for sorting different ideas

10. You need to leave a reminder for yourself for tomorrow morning. What do you do?

    a) Write a sticky note and put it where you'll see it
    b) Set a reminder on your phone
    c) Text yourself a recording so you don't forget
    d) Place a labeled index card on your desk

11. You're making a pros and cons list for a big decision. How do you do it?

   a) Handwrite the list in a journal
   b) Type it out in a Google Doc or notes app
   c) Speak your thoughts into a voice recording as you go for a walk
   d) Write pros/cons on separate cards and sort visually

12. You're collaborating with others on a shared project. How do you keep track of notes?

   a) Bring a shared notebook or pass around a written log
   b) Use a collaborative Google Doc or project management tool
   c) Record meetings or discussions to refer back to
   d) Use color-coded cards or sticky notes for team ideas

RESULTS: WHAT'S YOUR PREFERRED WRITING TOOL?

◆ Mostly A's – Handwriting Hero

You love writing things down by hand. Journals, sticky notes, and whiteboards are your best friends. The physical act of writing helps you think, remember, and create.

◆ Mostly B's – Digital Organizer

You're all about convenience, searchability, and syncing. From notes apps to shared docs, digital tools help you stay efficient, mobile, and ready for collaboration.

◆ Mostly C's – Audio Thinker

Your brain moves fast, and talking it out works best. Voice memos, dictation tools, and recordings keep up with your stream of consciousness and spontaneous ideas.

◆ Mostly D's – Visual Organizer

You like seeing and sorting ideas. Index cards, sticky notes, and movable boards help you to organize creatively, letting you reshape your work as it evolves.

Understanding your preferred writing style and tools can make the journey of writing your nonfiction book smoother, more enjoyable, and far more productive. Whether you're a handwritten planner, a digital organizer, an audio thinker, or a visual arranger, leaning into your natural strengths will help you stay motivated, organized, and creative. By choosing tools and strategies that align with how you already think and work, you'll set yourself up for success—and actually enjoy the process along the way.

6

REPURPOSING YOUR BOOK CONTENT

If you're writing a book, why not maximize its impact by repurposing your content on social media? Even before publication, you can use social media to build your audience, generate excitement, and give readers a taste of what's coming. Sharing snippets, insights, and behind-the-scenes moments can help you establish yourself as an authority in your niche and create a community eager to read your book when it launches.

TEN WAYS TO REPURPOSE YOUR BOOK CONTENT ON SOCIAL MEDIA

1. Share Short Quotes and Excerpts – Pull compelling quotes, intriguing passages, or engaging lines from your book and pair them with an eye-catching image or background to share on Instagram, Facebook, and Twitter.

2. Create Teaser Graphics – Use tools like Canva to create visually appealing teaser images featuring key messages or quotes from your book.

3. Turn Chapters into Blog Posts – Expand upon a section of your book and publish it as a blog post. Share the link on LinkedIn and Facebook to drive traffic to your website.

4. Go Live and Read an Excerpt – Host live reading sessions on Facebook, Instagram, or YouTube. Engage with your audience by discussing the inspiration behind the excerpt and answering their questions.

5. Develop a Mini-Series of Posts – Break down a chapter or theme into multiple social media posts that build upon each other, keeping your audience engaged over time.

6. Poll Your Audience – Use Instagram Stories, Facebook polls, or LinkedIn surveys to ask for feedback on book titles, cover designs, or specific content ideas.

7. Create Behind-the-Scenes Content – Show your writing process, workspace, research findings, or even funny moments that happened while working on your book.

8. Offer Free Downloadable Content – Provide a free chapter, worksheet, or resource related to your book to capture email subscribers and social media followers.

9. Engage with Themed Hashtags – Participate in trending or relevant hashtags such as #WritersLife, #BookLaunch, or #IndieAuthor to reach a wider audience.

10. Repurpose Content into Different Formats – Turn your content into videos, infographics, carousel posts, or audio snippets to appeal to different audiences across platforms.

QUIZ: WHICH SOCIAL MEDIA PLATFORM IS BEST FOR YOU AND YOUR BOOK?

Not all social media platforms are the same. Some are better suited for certain book genres, audiences, and author personalities. Take this quiz to determine the best platform for you!

1. What is the primary genre of your book?

    a) Business/Self-Help
    b) Fiction/Fantasy
    c) Romance/Drama
    d) Nonfiction/Educational

2. Who is your target audience?

    a) Professionals and entrepreneurs
    b) Young adults and fantasy lovers
    c) Romance enthusiasts and emotional readers
    d) Academics, researchers, or lifelong learners

3. How do you prefer to engage with your audience?

    a) Writing thoughtful articles or posts
    b) Sharing visual and creative content
    c) Interacting through conversations and storytelling
    d) Creating in-depth discussions or videos

4. Do you enjoy being on camera?

   a) Not really, I prefer writing
   b) Occasionally, if it's visually engaging
   c) Yes, especially for interactive chats
   d) Yes, I like sharing educational and/or entertaining content

5. How much time do you have for social media?

   a) I can dedicate time to writing posts weekly
   b) I enjoy making visuals and can post often
   c) I like chatting and engaging frequently
   d) I prefer deeper, long-form content occasionally

6. Do you like short, snappy content or long-form posts?

   a) Long-form insights
   b) A mix of both
   c) Short and engaging
   d) Detailed, informative posts

7. Are you comfortable with video content?

   a) Not my favorite
   b) I'll try short-form videos
   c) I love video interaction
   d) Yes, especially for tutorials

8. Where do you already have the most followers?

   a) LinkedIn
   b) Instagram

REPURPOSING YOUR BOOK CONTENT 193

    c) Facebook
    d) YouTube

9. Which social media platform are you likely to check when you have a moment?

    a) LinkedIn
    b) Instagram or TikTok
    c) Facebook
    d) YouTube

10. Which of the following engagements appeal to you?

    a) Professional groups and discussions
    b) Themed visual communities
    c) Interest groups and interactions
    d) Educational forums

11. What kind of media excites you most?

    a) Thoughtful discussions
    b) Beautiful visuals and reels
    c) Conversations and community building
    d) Video and in-depth tutorials

12. In what ways are you willing to invest time in building an audience?

    a) Through valuable insights
    b) Through engaging visuals
    c) Through conversations and shares
    d) Through video content

13. What's your goal with social media?

   a) To establish myself as a leader in my field
   b) To grow a visually engaging brand
   c) To build a reader community
   d) To educate and inform

14. How comfortable are you with analytics and tracking engagement?

   a) I analyze insights frequently
   b) I check trends but focus on creativity
   c) I track engagement casually
   d) I use analytics for growth

15. How do you define success on social media?

   a) Industry connections and credibility
   b) Viral content and aesthetics
   c) Loyal followers and discussions
   d) High engagement and video views

RESULTS: WHICH SOCIAL MEDIA PLATFORM IS BEST FOR YOU?

- **If you answered mostly A's: LinkedIn** – Best for business, self-help, and nonfiction authors looking to network and establish authority.

- **If you answered mostly B's: Instagram and TikTok** – Perfect for visually engaging fiction, fantasy, and lifestyle authors.

- **If you answered mostly C's: Facebook** – Ideal for romance, drama, and community-driven authors who love reader interaction.

- **If you answered mostly D's: YouTube** – Great for nonfiction, educational, and storytelling authors who enjoy video content.

By strategically repurposing your book content, you can engage your audience, establish credibility, and create anticipation for your book's launch, as well as remaining top-of-mind and connected to readers after your book is released. Start sharing today!

7
JUDGING YOUR BOOK BY ITS COVER

Your book cover is the first impression your audience will have of your non-fiction book, making it a crucial element in attracting the right readers. An effective cover should immediately communicate the book's subject, tone, and value proposition. For non-fiction, clarity is key—your title and subtitle should be easily readable, and your imagery should reinforce your book's core message. Whether you're writing a self-help guide, business book, memoir, or how-to manual, your cover design should align with industry expectations while standing out in a crowded marketplace. Colors, fonts, and imagery should evoke the right emotions; for example, a bold, clean design works well for business books, while memoirs often use personal, evocative photography. Researching top-selling books in your genre can provide valuable insights into what works while helping you identify opportunities to differentiate your cover.

Beyond aesthetics, your book cover must function well across various formats, from print editions to thumbnail-sized images on digital storefronts. A well-designed cover maintains its readability and impact even when scaled down. Additionally, investing in professional design can make a significant difference in credibility and sales potential. If you're working with a designer, provide them with a clear brief, including your book's target audience, key themes, and competitive titles. Testing different cover options with potential readers, through social media polls or A/B testing in ads, can provide valuable feedback before finalizing your design. A great cover doesn't just look good—it works as a strategic marketing tool, drawing in the right readers and making them want to explore what's inside.

CHECKLIST FOR CREATING AN EFFECTIVE NON-FICTION BOOK COVER

1. **Define your audience** – Identify who your book is for and what they expect from the cover.
2. **Research genre trends** – Check out successful covers in your target area to determine common elements.
3. **Craft a compelling title and subtitle** – Ensure they are clear, engaging, and easy to read.
4. **Choose the right typography** – Use fonts that match your book's tone (professional, playful, bold, etc.).
5. **Select a powerful color scheme** – Colors should align with your book's subject and evoke the right emotions.
6. **Use high-quality images or graphics** – And always be sure that the images your select are legally available.
7. **Ensure readability at all sizes** – Your title must be clear in both print and small online thumbnails.

8. **Hire a professional designer** – If possible, work with an experienced book cover designer.
9. **Include an engaging back cover** – For print books, compelling back cover text can influence buying decisions.
10. **Consider branding elements** – If you plan a series, ensure a consistent visual theme.
11. **Optimize for print and digital formats** – Ensure correct dimensions, resolution, and file formats for each platform.
12. **Check spine and margin requirements** – Print books need properly formatted spines and bleed areas.
13. **Test multiple designs** – Get feedback from readers, authors, or industry professionals before finalizing.
14. **Ensure genre-specific appeal** – Your cover should fit within industry norms while standing out.
15. **Finalize with a high-quality file** – Export in the correct formats (PDF for print, JPEG/PNG for digital).

By following these steps, you'll create a book cover that not only captures attention but also effectively sells your book to the right audience.

CRAFTING A COMPELLING TITLE/SUBTITLE

Here's a comparison of effective and ineffective book titles and subtitles, along with explanations of why they work (or don't).

1. Business and Entrepreneurship

✖ Weaker Title: *How to Work Less and Make More Money*

✓ Stronger Title: *The 4-Hour Workweek: Escape 9-5, Live Anywhere, and Join the New Rich*

Why? The stronger title is specific, intriguing, and presents a clear benefit. *4-Hour Workweek* grabs attention, while the subtitle gives concrete promises. The weaker title is vague and lacks a strong hook or credibility.

2. Self-Help and Personal Development

✘ Weaker Title: *Improve Your Habits and Change Your Life*

✓ Stronger Title: *Atomic Habits: An Easy and Proven Way to Build Good Habits and Break Bad Ones*

Why? *Atomic Habits* is unique, memorable, and suggests small, powerful changes. The subtitle reinforces credibility with "easy and proven." The weaker title is too broad, generic, and lacks specificity.

3. Health and Wellness

✘ Weaker Title: *Lose Weight and Get Healthy*

✓ Stronger Title: *The Obesity Code: Unlocking the Secrets of Weight Loss*

Why? *The Obesity Code* sounds authoritative and intriguing, while the subtitle suggests a scientific approach. The weaker title is overly generic and doesn't create curiosity or differentiation.

4. Memoir and Biography

✘ Weaker Title: *My Journey from Childhood to Success*

✓ Stronger Title: *Educated: A Memoir*

Why? *Educated* is a single, powerful word that encapsulates the memoir's theme. The weaker title is dull and doesn't hint at a compelling story.

5. Marketing and Business Strategy

✗ Weaker Title: *How to Make Your Ideas More Memorable*

✓ Stronger Title: *Made to Stick: Why Some Ideas Survive and Others Die*

Why? *Made to Stick* is catchy, metaphorical, and easy to remember. The subtitle creates intrigue. The weaker title is too plain and lacks an engaging hook.

6. Finance and Money Management

✗ Weaker Title: *Personal Finance 101: The Basics of Managing Your Money*

✓ Stronger Title: *I Will Teach You to Be Rich: No Guilt, No Excuses, Just a 6-Week Program That Works*

Why? The stronger title is bold, promising, and addresses objections (no guilt/excuses). The weaker title is bland, uninspiring, and doesn't create excitement.

7. Relationships and Psychology

✗ Weaker Title: *Understanding Relationships: How People Connect*

✓ Stronger Title: *Attached: The New Science of Adult Attachment and How It Can Help You Find – and Keep – Love*

Why? *Attached* is a short, compelling word, and the subtitle clarifies the subject with an intriguing promise. The weaker title is too vague and lacks an emotional pull.

8. Creativity and Writing

✗ Weaker Title: *How to Be More Creative in Your Life*

✓ Stronger Title: *Steal Like an Artist: 10 Things Nobody Told You About Being Creative*

Why? *Steal Like an Artist* is provocative and unexpected. The weaker title is generic and uninspiring.

KEY TAKEAWAYS FOR CRAFTING A STRONG TITLE AND SUBTITLE:

- **Be Specific** – Clearly state the benefit or topic.
- **Be Unique** – Avoid generic phrasing and make it stand out.
- **Create Intrigue** – A little mystery makes readers want to learn more.
- **Keep it Clear and Concise** – Don't overcomplicate the wording.

CHECKLIST AND QUESTIONS FOR CRAFTING THE PERFECT BOOK TITLE AND SUBTITLE

A strong book title and subtitle should be clear, compelling, and aligned with your audience's expectations while also standing out in the market. Use the checklist and guiding questions below to refine your title and subtitle for maximum impact.

Step 1: Identify Your Book's Core Message

- What is the main promise, transformation, or outcome for readers of your book?
- If your book could only communicate one big idea, what would it be?
- How would you summarize your book in a single sentence?

Step 2: Understand Your Audience and Market

- Who is your target reader, and what problem are they trying to solve?
- What emotions or desires do you want your title to evoke? (Curiosity, urgency, authority, inspiration, etc.)
- How do successful books in your genre title themselves? (Study bestsellers for patterns.)
- Does your title/subtitle match the tone and expectations of your genre?

Step 3: Craft a Strong, Memorable Title

- Does your title clearly convey the subject or benefit of your book?
- Is it short and easy to remember (ideally 2-5 words)?
- Does it have a unique or intriguing element to make it stand out?
- Does it use powerful, emotive, or unexpected words?
- Would it make someone curious enough to pick up your book?

Step 4: Create a Subtitle That Adds Value

- Does your subtitle clarify what your book is about?
- Does it highlight a specific benefit, method, or transformation?
- Does it answer the question: "Why should I read this book?"
- Does it use clear, direct language instead of vague phrasing?
- Does it include a sense of urgency, credibility, or authority?

Step 5: Test and Refine

- Say your title out loud—does it sound natural and compelling?
- Can someone understand your book's purpose just from the title and subtitle?
- Test multiple title options—do people find them intriguing and relevant?
- Get feedback from your target readers, authors, or industry professionals.
- Search your title online—does it stand out, or are there too many similar books?

By working through these questions and steps, you'll create a title and subtitle that grabs attention, resonates with readers, and sets your book up for success!

8

CRAFTING A WINNING DESCRIPTION

Your description is the second most important text you will write for your book, right after your title and subtitle. Use the following guide to help you to craft an effective book description, one that answers the right questions, speaks directly to the reader, and is easy to scan.

1. ANSWERS THE RIGHT QUESTIONS

Your description should make it immediately clear:

- Who this book is for – Identify your target reader. Are they entrepreneurs? Parents? Writers? Professionals looking to level up?
- What problem it solves – Clearly state the challenge or struggle your reader is facing. Are they trying to grow their business? Improve their mindset? Write a bestselling book?
- What results they can expect – Show them the transformation. Will they gain confidence? Sell

more? Reduce stress? Give them a reason to take action.

Example: *If you've ever struggled with marketing your book and felt overwhelmed by all the advice out there, this guide simplifies the process so you can sell more books without the confusion.*

For your own book, fill in your own answers to the questions below:

a) Who is this book for?

Describe your target reader in the space below. Be sure to include such identifiers as age, genre, job/life stage, etc. where appropriate.

_____

_____

_____

b) What problem does your book solve?

What is the challenge facing your potential readers?

_____

_____

_____

Describe how your book will help them to face their challenges.

_____

_____

_____

c) What results can your reader expect?

Describe below how your reader and/or their situation will be different once they embrace the message of your book.

_____

_____

_____

2. THE POWER OF YOU

Your reader needs to feel like this book was written for them. Instead of distant, impersonal language, speak directly to them using "you." For example:

In this book, you'll discover simple strategies to grow your audience, sell more books, and build a long-term author business.

Be sure to avoid impersonal language, such as: This book provides strategies for audience growth, increased sales, and long-term success for authors.

3. MAKE IT SCANNABLE

Most readers scan book descriptions rather than reading every word. Help them absorb the key points quickly by using:

- Short paragraphs for easy readability
- Bolded or underlined text for emphasis
- Bullet points to highlight takeaways

Example:

Inside, you'll learn how to:

- *Identify and attract your **ideal readers***
- *Set up an **easy system** for selling books directly*
- *Use **social media** without feeling overwhelmed*
- *Build a sustainable author business that keeps growing*

By structuring your description with these elements, you'll grab attention, create connection, and boost book sales.

Taking all of these points together, work on filling in the following template:

Catchy opening line:

_____

_____

_____

Speak about point #1—address your target reader, their problem, and how your book will solve it. (Be sure to use "you" language—as in point #2, and bullet points/bold/italics, as in point #3.):

_____

_____

_____

_____

_____

_____

_____

Mention a comparison statement ("if you like _____ you'll love _____"):

If you already have any reviews or endorsements, add them here:

Close with a strong call-to-action statement:

_____

_____

_____

_____

_____

_____

Crafting your **book blurb**—a one- or two-sentence description that you can easily state in conversations—can borrow elements from your book description. However, it should be much shorter—literally a sentence or two—and it will be spoken, not written, so it must be easy to say and hear.

Try crafting your book blurb below. It may take several tries to get it down to something easy—and quick—to say that retains your topic area and enthusiasm.

_____

_____

_____

_____

_____

9
POINTS ABOUT PUBLISHING

You wrote the book—now what? Well, you can certainly opt to just hit PRINT on your computer, run off a copy or two, and staple the pages together. Many authors do exactly that—passing along their printed copies to family and friends and printing them as needed.

On the other hand, if you want your manuscript to look, feel, and smell like a "real" book, you'll need:

- Editing of the manuscript
- Book/page layout, including margins, gutters, chapter headings, pagination, front and back matter, and more
- Cover art and layout, both a front-only cover for digital, as well as a wrap-around cover for print
- Coordination and optimization of interior graphics
- Formatting/file conversion for eBooks and print
- Submission to international online and off-line book stores and libraries

- ISBN numbers
- Bar codes
- Library of Congress designations
- Book printing
- And more!

These items—and more—amount to what is described as publishing your book, so let's look at the different options an author has in book publishing.

TRADITIONAL PUBLISHING

Book Digest defines traditional publishing as "when a publisher offers the author a contract and, in turn, prints, publishes, and sells the book through booksellers and other retailers. The publisher ... pays (the author) royalties from the sales."

Traditional publishers play a vital role in the creation and distribution of a tremendous number of books each year. Of course, along with all of the time—and expense—of transforming a book from mere words on a page to a "living, breathing book" in the hands of a potential reader, there are certain requirements and stipulations that come along with working within the "traditional" publishing world. Some things to consider include:

- Publishers need to make money, too, and in order that they at least cover their expenses, they're looking to work with authors who have an established following and a strong probability of selling many books—at least 10,000+ books. (On a side note, the "average" book sells less than 250

copies per year/less than 3,000 copies over its lifetime!)
- Publishers make money when books sell, so the expected royalty to an author averages about 15%.
- All creative rights to a book belong to the publishers, as they have the final say over the cover design, title, and even text on the pages.
- If, by chance, a person wishes to make a movie of your book or some other additional distribution, you do not necessarily have the right to make such deals, as the publisher may retain all rights.
- Publishers have the right to take as much time as they want in bringing a book to market, and may even abandon a particular book project altogether, while still tying up all of the book's rights.

However, on the positive side:

- Professional publishers are professional because ... well, they have knowledge and connections that you can only dream about! Having guided hundreds—if not thousands—of books from mere text to publishing success stories, traditional publishers certainly know their market and how to leverage it to their best advantage.
- If your book is accepted by a traditional publisher, there will be NO cost to you. In fact, you may even receive an advance on future royalties!
- Having a team of professionals means that while creative decisions are out of your hands, they are in the hands of people who have done this over and over

again, and thus are likely to be in a better, more objective, place to offer opinions.
- Publishers know people—from artists, editors, and layout directors to readers, reviewers, and those in charge of distribution channels. Their reach is far beyond what you could imagine in the book world.
- Working with a traditional publisher is the ultimate goal for many writers desiring to leave their book in the hands of experts who will guide it ultimately—hopefully!—to success.

Before even submitting any queries to a traditional publisher, an author should research the publisher to learn whether such a partnership would be a good fit, including questions such as:

- What types of books are represented by this publisher?
- Does the publisher have a particular mission? And if so, does it align with my own mission and values?
- Does the publisher represent authors like myself—perhaps in age, genre, or book goal?

Once accepted by a traditional publisher, be sure to get clarification regarding the following:

- Do I retain the rights to my book? Which rights? For example, if approached by a movie production company, do I retain the right to agree (and profit) from such a venture, or does this contract give all future rights to the publisher?

- Will my creative input be accepted and respected regarding my book?
- Do I have any say in pricing, distribution, or promotional placements? Will appearances be required of me, and if so, do I have a right of refusal?

These questions should also be asked of a hybrid publisher, as well as any other book contracts an author may enter into.

While "selling lots of books" may be the ultimate goal for many authors, there are plenty of other reasons a person may desire to write and publish a book, including:

- for creative fulfillment
- to insure the preservation of a family history
- to promote and further a business or career
- to use in workshops or training sessions that you deliver
- to sell at seminars and when delivering speeches
- to preserve and distribute a memoir of a family member
- to collect recipes, tips or other materials—for fun, profit, or to celebrate a milestone

These are all wonderful reasons to write a book, but unfortunately, since the benefits that come along with book publication in these cases are not dependent upon book sales, a traditional publisher would not gain financially and would therefore not be interested in taking on such a project. In former times, that would signal the end of your book right there, but fortunately, we live in times when there exist other options to bring your book to publication aside from traditional publishing houses.

SELF-PUBLISHING

What do Benjamin Franklin, William Blake, Walt Whitman, and Virginia Woolf have in common? How about the best seller *The Joy of Cooking*? Give up? Well, not only have you heard of them all—some hundreds of years later—but they were all self-published! Can you imagine Walt Whitman getting turned down by publishers? If you've been there, you now know that you're in good company!

Self-publishing has been around since the dawn of the Gutenberg printing press, and the prevalence of computers in our homes has only served to make self-publishing more accessible to all. By opting for self-publishing, you would retain all rights, royalties, and artistic decisions. Of course, along with all of those benefits come responsibilities as well, especially if you want to be sure that your book doesn't look "homemade."

You will also need to consider the following:

- Where will you publish your book? On Amazon? Kobo? Kindle Unlimited? Which is the best choice for you?
- Who will print your book? What is the cost per book, as well as the minimum "run" necessary to get your book published? Will you need to mail out your book as orders are received, or will it be "print-on-demand" as orders come in? Do you want paperback or hard-cover books?

- How will you distribute your book? Are you planning to have it available in bookstores or solely online? How about a book launch party or book-signing event?
- Do you need an ISBN number and bar code? A Library of Congress designation? A copyright?
- Will you be promoting your book? Striving for book reviews? Distributing your book in other ways?

While self-publishing your book can be the ultimate Do-It-Yourself project, it certainly isn't for the faint of heart. It can be great fun for those comfortable with various apps, programs, and file formats and who have 100+ hours to devote to cover design, editing, book formatting, layout, file conversions, distribution, promotion, and the myriad of other decisions that will come your way. Realistically speaking, self-publication will generally cost between $200-$5,000, depending on the cost and use of editors, book cover designers, print layout professionals, and distributors. While you can skip all professional help and go at it alone, you certainly may find yourself spending hundreds of hours and still ending up with a homemade, badly written or designed book.

Self-Publishing Companies

There are plenty of companies around who charge just for services you need in order to assist you in self-publishing your book. From page layout and file formats to templates for cover designs and print-on-demand, many companies exist online where you can simply upload your book document, follow the steps, and pay for what you need. There are also many editors who will guide you through the self-publishing process, employing additional professionals (at your expense) if needed.

Self-publishing a book is certainly a way to be intimately involved in every single decision in the development of your book. While technology has certainly made self-publication an incredibly viable solution, it still may not be for everyone. However, if you are comfortable with various types of software and aren't quick to stress when the details—and responsibility for decisions—take off, self-publication is certainly a great way to guide your book your way—every step of the way!

HYBRID PUBLISHING

What are hybrid publishers? Hybrid publishers are just like traditional publishers, except that in hybrid publishing, the author will partner in subsidizing the cost of publication. The publisher will manage the editing, book layout, proofing, cover design, the ISBN, printing costs, review copies, book distribution and marketing. This marketing could include things like gathering contacts and networking with them on your behalf, setting up signings for you, looking into advertising, adding books to various databases (wholesalers, bookshops) creating banners, bookmarks, hosting giveaways, writing blog posts and various social media work for you.

When choosing a hybrid publisher, consider the following guidelines from the Independent Book Publishers Association. A hybrid publisher should:

- **Define a mission and vision for its publishing program.** At Red Penguin Books, our mission is to empower authors to achieve their publication goals.

We firmly believe in "changing lives, one book at a time" and take pride in partnering with authors from around the globe and in all walks of life from start to print, bringing their stories, messages, and ideas to the world through digital, print, and audiobook publication.

- **Vet submissions.** Authors who submit their work for consideration to Red Penguin Books should have a clear sense of vision with their writing, along with publishing goals that align with our own. Submissions are evaluated based on different criteria depending on the author's personal, professional, and publication goals, and we are proud to work with authors of all genres.
- **Publish under its own imprint(s) and ISBNs.** We are not a "self-publishing assistance"—at Red Penguin Books, we publish under our own imprints.
- **Publish to industry standards.** Industry standards are important to us at Red Penguin Books, and while some books—such as poetry and art books—may require their own particulars, all adhere to publication standards and requirements.
- **Ensure editorial, design, and production quality.** Our books go through several edits along their path to publication, including line edits, formatting edits, and two complete print-outs to literally "red pen" the copies, as there is nothing quite like having paper in hand to make edits.
- **Provide distribution services.** As our authors each have different publication and distribution goals, Red Penguin Books has worked to get our authors' books placed everywhere from bookstores and libraries to

specialty stores, schools, medical offices, and major organizations.
- **Demonstrate respectable sales.** Along with book sales, we are proud that our authors have won many book awards, attained #1 New Release status, and have watched their rankings—and sales numbers—grow. Our book sales—and successes—come from a variety of sources, including online platforms, brick-and-mortar bookstores, specialty shops, educational organizations, corporate sales, and licensing. Authors also profit from wholesale print book sales and digital sales through their own websites, which we can help set up for them. Each author is different, and we strive to get their books to the best possible channels to achieve their goals.
- **Pay authors a higher-than-standard royalty.** We offer exceptionally generous royalty splits, ensuring authors receive a larger share of the proceeds—as they rightfully deserve. With fewer "middlemen" such as book agents, our authors can better benefit from the fruits of their labor.

We are fortunate to live—and write—at a time where there are many options in regards to publishing. No one method is the best for every book or every author. In fact, many authors have utilized different methods for different books that they write, knowing that there are advantages to each. The key is to stay informed, stay flexible, and choose the path that best serves your book, your goals, and your unique voice—because in today's publishing landscape, you truly have the power to decide how your story reaches the world.

10
IT'S TIME TO CELEBRATE!

What do you want to do to celebrate your book release? At the very least, you deserve a party, a toast to your success, and the opportunity to share your joy and sign some books! Before we get to the professional events you should consider, I want you to think about what YOU want to do to celebrate this momentous occasion. Too often, we only celebrate major life milestones—like marriage or having babies—that involve other people, or accolades bestowed upon us by others, such as graduations or workplace awards. Publishing a book is just as significant as these milestones, yet too often, people hesitate to brag or call attention to themselves by celebrating this amazing achievement. But believe me, it is a well-earned accomplishment, and it deserves recognition.

So, definitely plan something with family and friends—please do not hide your joy in a sea of modesty! However, if you—like the authors in our story—wrote your book to ignite your business, be sure to plan book release events that will give your book and your business the boost you desire. Below is a checklist of general book release strategies you should embrace, along with ideas for book events to continue exposing your book and business to new audiences.

CREATE A MEDIA KIT/PRESS RELEASE

You'll want to have something prepared—both to announce your new book to your contacts and to use when reaching out to podcasts, libraries, bookstores, and other opportunities. A media kit should be at least one page long, sent as a PDF, and include:

- Your book cover image
- Book description
- ISBN numbers
- Book reviews (if available)
- Your author bio and photo

EMAIL ANNOUNCEMENTS

When your book releases, prepare an email to send to all of your contacts. This should include:

- A picture of your book cover
- A description in the body of your email
- A media kit attachment
- Any in-person book events (including details in the email announcements)

Additionally, update your email signature line to include a picture of your book cover linked to a purchase page.

LINKEDIN STRATEGIES

If LinkedIn is an important part of your audience-building strategy, be sure to consider the following book release actions:

- Include "author of _____" in your headline.
- Change your profile picture to one of you holding your book.

Create multiple posts about your book:

○ Day 1: Announce your book release.

○ Day 2: Post a gratitude message thanking and tagging people who helped you.

○ Day 3: Share a sample from your book (e.g., a chapter or introduction).

○ Day 4: Share a book review and tag the reviewer.

○ Ongoing: Post book reviews/testimonials, notices about book events, and podcast appearances.

This posting strategy can also be applied to other social media platforms. Adjust the tone and format to fit each platform while maintaining consistency in messaging.

PODCAST APPEARANCES

Being a podcast guest is a great way to promote your business and book. Find podcasts that align with your message and send your media kit along with a letter of introduction to podcast hosts. Check each podcast's website for application forms. Expect some rejections, acceptances, and nonresponses. Once booked, maximize exposure by making multiple posts:

- When you're booked: Thank and tag the host.
- On the recording day: Share behind-the-scenes insights.
- When the episode airs: Promote the interview and encourage engagement.

GETTING INTO LIBRARIES

Getting your book into libraries involves outreach, marketing, and distribution efforts. Be sure of the following:

1. ISBN and Cataloging

- Your book must have an International Standard Book Number (ISBN), essential for library cataloging.
- Your book must be cataloged with the Library of Congress Classification.

2. Distribution to Library Suppliers

- Your book should be available through Baker & Taylor and Ingram Content Group.

3. Direct Library Outreach

- Contact local libraries and provide them with a copy of your book, a press release, and other relevant information.
- Attend library events, book fairs, or author readings.

- Engage with librarians via social media.
- Offer special discounts or incentives for libraries to purchase your book.
- Consider donating a copy to local libraries to increase awareness and potential future purchases.

Persistence is key—building relationships within the library community takes time.

BOOKSTORES

Bookstores can be wonderful venues for book launch events. However, keep in mind that bookstores are businesses and may have requirements, such as:

- A minimum 55% discount off the retail price
- A required minimum number of attendees or book buyers
- Specific event timing, such as only hosting events on the book's release day

Understanding each bookstore's policies will help determine if it's a good fit for your event. If aligned, a bookstore event can be a great opportunity to celebrate, engage readers, and generate fantastic social media content.

LONG-TERM BOOK PROMOTION

Remember, a book release isn't just a one-day event—you will be promoting your book for years to come. While it's great to ride the initial momentum of your release, don't feel pressured to do everything at once. Even if you start promoting later, it's never too late to share your book with the world. Stay consistent, keep engaging your audience, and celebrate every milestone along the way!

PART THREE
A-Z BOOK IDEAS
A GUIDE FOR ENTREPRENEURS AND EXPERTS

Inspiration for Every Industry

Not sure what to write about? Part 3 of *Bookology* is your personal idea bank—an A-to-Z guide packed with creative book concepts tailored to dozens of different professions. Whether you're an accountant, a yoga instructor, a florist, or a financial planner, you'll find ready-to-use inspiration that speaks directly to your field, audience, and expertise.

Each entry offers book ideas designed to build your authority, attract ideal clients, and help you stand out in a crowded market. If you've ever thought, "I want to write a book, but I don't know where to start," this section is your launchpad.

Accountant

- A book of questions, checklists, and fill-in-the-blanks to prepare for taxes and financial milestones.
- Collaborative book: *A Lifetime in Accounting*—chapters by experts on finances for major life events (marriage, homeownership, college, retirement, etc.).
- *Small Business Tax Guide*—demystifying deductions, audits, and financial best practices.

Actor

- A candid account of audition life, rejections, and wins.
- A book of monologues for stage actors.
- A workbook for teens entering the performing arts world.

Acupuncturist

- A history, applications, and success stories of acupuncture.
- *The A-Z Guide to Acupressure*—self-care techniques for stress relief and pain management.

Administrative Aide

- *101 Productivity Hacks from a Professional Administrator.*
- *The Executive Assistant's Playbook*—organizing schedules, managing teams, and handling crises.

Airline Pilot

- A memoir of life in the skies, from takeoff to turbulence.
- A children's adventure book about learning to fly.
- A behind-the-scenes guide to how aviation really works.

Animal Trainer

- Stories of training pets and working animals.
- A guide to housebreaking your pet—without losing your mind!
- Collaborative book: *The Ultimate Pet Guide*, with input from a veterinarian, an animal nutritionist, and a professional groomer.

Anthropologist

- A children's book about cultures of the world (or a region), including traditions, rituals, and hidden gems.
- A book exploring diverse customs and their significance.

Architect

- A photo-heavy book showing before-and-after residential transformations with expert design tips.
- A beginner's guide to understanding blueprints and building plans.
- A fictional children's story where the main character builds fantastical cities.

Artist

- A coffee table art book showcasing the artist's work.
- A children's book on art techniques, illustrated with the artist's own work.
- A guide for selling art online and managing your art career.

Astronomer

- A calendar book of events in the sky to observe over the next five years.
- A beginner's guide to observing the night sky.
- A children's book demystifying celestial phenomena.

Athlete

- A sports-themed children's picture book promoting perseverance.
- A cookbook for high-performance eating on a budget.
- Collaborative book: *Secrets from Athletic Pros*, with fitness trainers, nutritionists, and sports psychologists.

Baker

- Baking Terms and Techniques: *An A-Z Glossary*.
- *52 Weeks of Cakes and Pastries*: A Yearlong Baking Guide.
- A cozy mystery novel series set in a bakery.

Banker

- A-to-Z terms in banking, economics, and finance.
- A book on personal finance and investment strategies.

Barber

- A grooming and self-care guide for young men.
- A-Z of Classic and Modern Hairstyles.
- A children's book about a boy's first haircut.

Bartender

- A cocktail recipe book organized by emotion or occasion.
- A humorous memoir of life behind the bar.
- Collaborative book: *Drink and Dine*, featuring drinks paired with chef-curated meals.

Beautician

- Skin care tips for every age.
- Make-up through the decades: looks and techniques.

Biologist

- An accessible science book on animal adaptations for curious kids.
- A deep dive into how ecosystems bounce back after disasters.
- A guided nature journal for hikers and explorers.

Bus Driver

- Driving tips from a professional driver.
- A collection of humorous and heartwarming passenger stories.
- A children's book about a bus—starring the bus.

Business Coach

- A strategic goal-setting guide for creative entrepreneurs.
- A collection of transformational client case studies.
- A DIY branding workbook with exercises and checklists.

Carpenter

- *A-Z Guide to Hardware and Tools.*
- *Before and After: A Picture Book of Home Renovations.*
- A book of meditative reflections comparing life to woodworking.

Chef

- *A-Z of Ingredients and Cooking Tools.*
- 52 seasonal recipes for Sunday dinners throughout the year.
- A kids' cookbook with simple recipes and cooking skills.

Child Care Provider

- A pocket-sized journal for tracking childhood memories.
- *A-Z Guide of Must-Read Children's Books.*
- Collaborative book, with insights from pediatricians, teachers, and psychologists.

Chiropractor

- A posture and spinal health guide for desk workers.
- A wellness book integrating chiropractic care and holistic health.
- A case-study based book showing real patient transformations.

Clergy

- A book of blessings for every occasion.
- A spiritual reflection journal.
- A children's book about a religious observance.

Coach

- A goal-setting planner rooted in the author's coaching framework.
- A leadership book built around lessons learned from coaching.
- A workbook for teens on building resilience and self-confidence.

Comedian

- A mix of memoir and humor-writing tips.
- A children's book of jokes.

Consultant

- *My Signature Success Plan*—multi-step strategies for personal or business growth.
- Lessons from my clients: case studies in success.
- A workbook/journal for recording progress and growth.

Counselor/Therapist

- A self-help book on healing from anxiety or trauma.
- A fictionalized novel based on common emotional growth journeys.
- A guided journal with prompts based on therapeutic methods.

Cryptographer

- The history of cryptography and cybersecurity.
- A deep dive into the evolution of secret codes.
- A children's book written in a simple code (with clues to crack it, of course!).

Dancer

- A book about dance around the world.
- A workout book for non-dancers.
- A children's book about becoming a dancer.

Data Scientist

- A book of interesting statistics in a favorite area.
- A book on how data is used in business, politics, and everyday life.

Dentist

- A parent's guide to children's dental care, from baby teeth to braces.
- A children's book about a first trip to the dentist.
- 101 fascinating facts about teeth.

Designer (Fashion, Interior, Graphic, etc.)

- A book exploring the principles of good design.
- A workbook for planning home design/renovations.

Dietitian

- A nutrition guide for people with specific health goals (e.g., managing diabetes).
- A myth-busting book about popular diet trends.
- A recipe collection organized by body-supporting goals (energy, immunity, digestion).

Diver (Commercial or Marine Biologist)

- A memoir of an especially exciting/terrifying event.
- A photography book with uniques photos from under the sea.
- A children's book about how pollution is affecting the oceans.

DJ

- A music lover's memoir of life behind the booth.
- A how-to book on building a DJ brand and getting gigs.
- A photo/music history book chronicling club and dance culture.

Doctor

- *Keeping Track of Your Health*: a medical journal for patients.
- Longevity secrets: a collaborative book with advice from medical experts.
- A children's book dispelling fears of doctors and shots.

Dog Trainer

- A behavior-specific training manual (e.g., for anxious or aggressive dogs).
- A picture book from a dog's point of view learning new tricks.
- A journal-style book to track progress in training your pet.

Driver

- A memoir of wild, heartwarming, or strange rides.
- A book of lessons learned about human nature from the front seat.
- A guide to turning ride-share driving into a profitable side hustle.

Editor

- A-Z guide to commonly misspelled words.
- *Grammar Gone Wild*: hilarious writing mistakes.
- A book on editing for aspiring writers.

Educator

- *Test Prep and Study Guide for SAT, ACT*, etc.
- A classroom survival guide for first-year teachers.
- A collection of real stories that celebrate moments of impact in teaching.

Electrician

- A DIY home safety and electrical basics manual for homeowners.
- A children's book about how electricity works, told in a fun narrative.
- A career guide for those entering the trades, with stories and steps to get licensed.

Engineer

- A memoir chronicling the author's experiences on the most interesting engineering projects of their career.
- A children's book on engineering marvels and innovations.
- A practical book on solving real-world problems using engineering principles.

Entrepreneur

- Case studies/stories from fellow entrepreneurs.
- A book on starting and growing a business.

Esthetician

- A skincare guide organized by age, skin type, and concerns.
- A beauty memoir sharing behind-the-scenes client transformations.
- A planner or journal for tracking skincare routines and results.

Event Planner

- An event planning guide, with checklists and planning pages.
- Tips for planning weddings, corporate events, and milestone celebrations.
- A book of wild stories of the unexpected happening at an event.

Farmer

- A seasonal guide to home gardening and sustainable practices.
- A memoir chronicling the ups and downs of life on the land.
- A children's book introducing where food comes from.

Fashion Designer

- A visual book of sketches and the story behind each design.
- A DIY sewing and fashion design workbook for beginners.
- A coffee table book on fashion evolution through the decades.

Filmmaker

- A comprehensive, behind-the-scenes dive into the art and craft of film production.
- A children's book on making movies from concept to screen.

Financial Advisor

- *52 Weeks to Financial Freedom*: a yearlong money plan.
- *Smart Money Moves*: A guide to financial independence.
- A teen guide to basic money principles.

Firefighter

- A behind-the-scenes memoir of bravery, teamwork, and adrenaline.
- A first responder mental health guide for stress and trauma recovery.
- A children's book about fire safety.

Flight Attendant

- A travel memoir of life in the skies.
- A practical book of travel hacks and insider tips.
- A fiction romance or mystery series set on different flights/airports.

Florist

- A comprehensive guide to the meaning of flowers throughout history and across cultures.
- A photo book of famous bouquets and iconic gardens.
- A floral design how-to book with visual step-by-steps.

Gardener

- A visual guide to garden pests and problems.
- A month-by-month gardening guide by region.
- A journal-style book for garden planning, tracking, and sketching.

Geologist

- A children's guide to Earth's history.
- A travel book on the geology behind natural landmarks.
- A field journal-style book for rock collectors and amateur scientists.

Grant Writer

- A step-by-step guide to writing winning grant proposals.
- A book for non-profits on diversifying funding beyond grants.
- A collaborative anthology of success stories from funded projects.

Graphic Designer

- 101 great logos and what we can learn from them.
- A practical workbook for non-designers about logos, branding, and visual storytelling.
- A creative inspiration book of typography and color palettes.

Guidance Counselor/Job Coach

- A book of questions for college planning.
- A practical workbook on resumé building, interviews, and career pivots.
- A career guidebook for teens exploring post-high-school options.

Guitarist

- A beginner's guide to chords, rhythm, and songwriting.
- A memoir from the road: life as a gigging musician.
- A children's picture book on learning music with a lovable guitar character.

Hairdresser

- A-Z guide to hair care and styling.
- A memoir sharing funny, heartwarming salon stories.
- A DIY hair care guide for teens or curly-haired clients.

Health Care Worker/Health Coach

- A simplified dictionary of common medical terms.
- A 30-day habit-building guide for wellness and energy.
- A guided journal with daily prompts around mindset, food, and movement.

Historian

- The story of a lesser-known historical figure or event brought to life.
- A historical fiction novel based on the author's area of expertise.
- A children's book about a little-known—but rather important—historical event.

Home Organizer

- A room-by-room decluttering workbook with templates and checklists.
- A home organization planner for busy families.
- A mindset-based guide: emotional blocks behind clutter and how to overcome them.

Human Resources Manager

- A practical guide for job seekers, offering an insider's perspective on how to stand out in a competitive market.
- A business book on creating people-first workplace cultures.
- A compilation of funny or awkward workplace interactions.

Insurance/Investment Advisor

- A guide to insurance needs at every stage of life.
- A finance guide for first-time investors or young professionals.
- A collaborative book featuring stories of clients who achieved financial freedom.

Interior Designer

- A DIY home styling book based on personality types.
- A design diary following the transformation of one space from start to finish.

- A visual guide to mixing patterns, textures, and color with confidence.

Interpreter

- A memoir of crossing cultures and languages in real-world settings.
- A bilingual children's book told in two languages side-by-side.

IT Professional

- *The A-to-Z Tech Troubleshooting Guide.*
- A fictional tech-thriller written by someone who knows the inside scoop.
- Cybersecurity and online safety for kids.

Janitor/Custodian

- A humorous and heartwarming memoir about this unsung hero's view of the world.
- A children's book celebrating school or hospital custodians.
- A guide to cleaning the uncleanable.

Jeweler

- A-Z guide to jewelry and gemstones.
- A memoir with tales of custom pieces and personal stories.
- A children's guide to gemstones.

Jockey

- *What I Learned on the Back of a Horse*—a book of reflections.
- A guidebook on horse racing and training.
- A children's book about a young wanna-be jockey.

Journalist

- A memoir-style behind-the-scenes look at covering major news events.
- A book exploring the ethics and challenges of modern journalism.
- A writing guide for young, aspiring journalists, with real-world reporting prompts.

Judge

- A legal education book demystifying courtroom processes for the public.
- A memoir of memorable, moving, or absurd cases.
- A justice-themed children's book about fairness and truth.

Karate Instructor

- A character-building guide using martial arts philosophy for kids and teens.
- A memoir of discipline, dojo life, and life lessons from martial arts.

- An illustrated history book on the origins and forms of martial arts.

Kindergarten Teacher

- A guide for parents on preparing kids for kindergarten success.
- A children's book about the first day of school.
- A picture book series teaching social-emotional learning concepts.

Kitchen Designer

- A guide to creating functional, beautiful kitchens for every budget.
- A before-and-after photo book with layout tips and inspiration.
- A workbook for planning your dream kitchen (sketch pages, checklists, vision boards).

Kinesiologist

- A sports recovery book for amateur athletes and fitness enthusiasts.
- A posture and mobility manual for people who sit all day.

K9 Trainer (Police or Service Dogs)

- A book detailing the life and training of a service or working dog.
- A children's story following a puppy in training to become a hero dog.

- A manual for training emotional support dogs at home.

Landscaper

- A practical guide to designing sustainable and beautiful outdoor spaces.
- A photo-rich idea book with regional planting suggestions.
- A children's book about garden creatures.

Lawyer

- A myth-busting book about legal rights and courtroom drama.
- A step-by-step estate planning workbook for families.
- A fiction novel based on composite cases and courtroom intrigue.
- The five most common legal questions about _____ [your specialty].
- Collaborative book, along with specialists in estate planning, business law, family law, etc.

Librarian

- 101 search tips and online resources.
- A guide to setting up home or classroom libraries with kid-friendly systems.
- A children's book where the librarian is the magical guide to adventure.

Lighting Designer

- Lighting your home—tips from a professional lighting designer.
- A book on the impact of lighting in theater, film, and events.
- A children's book about all the behind-the-scenes people at a show.

Marketing Consultant

- A small business marketing playbook for solopreneurs.
- A branding workbook with step-by-step exercises to define your voice.

Massage Therapist

- Self-massage and relaxation techniques for busy people.
- A self-care guide to stretching, posture, and body awareness.
- A collection of client transformation stories.

Midwife

- A guide for expectant parents on natural childbirth and options.
- A memoir of powerful birth stories from the delivery room.

- A journal-style pregnancy tracker from a midwife's perspective.

Musician

- A memoir about life on tour, in the studio, or chasing the dream.
- A songwriting journal with prompts and blank sheet music.
- A children's picture book introducing musical instruments and rhythm.

Mechanic

- *Car Care 101*: a guide to maintaining your vehicle.
- A children's book on basic vehicle parts and operation.
- A memoir with stories from the shop and roadside rescues.

Meteorologist

- A guide to understanding forecasting and climate change.
- A children's picture book on weather.
- A photo book of wild weather worldwide.

Nanny

- A caregiver's handbook with child development milestones and tips.

- A sweet children's book about a beloved nanny's magical days.
- A guide for new nannies entering the profession.

Nonprofit Director

- A guide to building and funding a mission-driven organization.
- A collection of impact stories from the field.
- A workbook for non-profit boards and strategic planning.

Notary Public

- An A-to-Z guide to notarization, legal forms, and industry tips.
- A picture book for children explaining what a notary does and why they're important through kid-friendly language.

Novelist

- A behind-the-scenes look at writing and publishing a novel.
- A workbook to help other writers outline and plan their novels.
- A children's book of simple writing prompts.

Numismatist (Coin Collector)

- A collector's guide to rare coins.
- Resources and tips for amateur coin collectors.

- A children's book that introduces young readers to the fascinating world of coin collecting.

Nurse

- A home first-aid handbook.
- A wellness guide for nurses on burnout, boundaries, and balance.
- A children's book about a trip to the hospital to help kids understand what to expect and ease their fears.

Nutritionist

- A myth-busting nutrition book for real-life eating habits.
- A health tracker and food journal with tips for each goal (energy, skin, digestion).
- A guide to healthy eating on-the-go for teens or young adults.

Occupational Therapist

- Collaborative book featuring physical, speech, and art therapists.
- A practical book on motor skills and daily routines for kids with developmental delays.
- A toolkit for caregivers with home-based OT activities.

Office Manager

- A handbook for creating calm, productive, people-first office environments.
- A planner or journal for staying organized and managing multiple tasks.
- A humorous book about office life told through anecdotes and characters.

Oncologist

- A book for patients and families navigating a cancer diagnosis.
- A memoir with deeply human stories of strength, loss, and resilience.
- A children's book about a family member with cancer.

Optometrist

- A guide to maintaining eye health at any age.
- An A-to-Z guide to eye care, vision correction, and common conditions.
- A children's book on what to expect at your first eye exam.

Ornithologist

- A beautifully illustrated book on birdwatching.
- A guide to bird physiology and behavior.
- A children's book about a lost bird.

Orthodontist

- A teen-friendly book on braces and self-confidence.
- A guide for parents on supporting their child through orthodontic treatment.
- A visual book comparing various types of orthodontic technology.

Painter

- A-Z guide to home painting and color selection.
- A collaborative book with a decorator, carpenter, and electrician.
- A children's book about painting their room.

Perfumer

- The sources and technology behind the creation of popular scents.
- A children's book about making perfumes.
- The meaning behind different scents.

Personal Trainer

- *Fitness for Every Age and Stage of Life.*
- A 30-day fitness and habit journal with coaching tips.
- A motivational guide for starting and sticking to movement routines.

Photographer

- A photo memoir of a community or a personal journey.
- A book on building a photography business from hobby to pro.
- A book on photography techniques and storytelling.

Physical Therapist

- A guide to injury prevention and recovery for everyday people.
- A how-to book on mobility and pain relief at home.
- A collection of client case studies with functional movement plans.

Plumber

- A children's book about how plumbing works.
- A DIY handbook on basic plumbing repairs and maintenance.

Police Officer

- A children's book about how police keep us safe.
- 50 tips on personal safety.
- A fictionalized story of a wild case.

Quantum Physicist

- A popular science book explaining quantum concepts through real-world analogies.
- A thought-provoking book on quantum physics and the nature of reality.
- A fictional story based on quantum concepts (multiverse, entanglement).

Quilter

- A pattern book featuring original quilt designs and inspiration.
- A memoir told through quilts and the stories behind them.
- A children's book about a magical quilt passed through generations.

Radiologist

- *Inside the Body*—photos of wild images caught on scans.
- A children's book explaining X-rays, MRIs, and CT scans.
- An adult book explaining the different types of scans and uses.

Realtor

- A homebuyer's guide for first-timers, step by step.
- A book on staging, curb appeal, and prepping for sale.

- A memoir of surprising, emotional, or hilarious real estate stories.

Roofer

- A book on home maintenance from the roof down.
- A contractor's guide to customer relationships and business growth.
- A visual book on historic and creative roofing styles around the world.

Salesperson

- Scripts, emails, and pitches from a successful salesperson.
- Stories from the sales floor—the craziest things to happen in retail.

Scientist

- A "science for the curious" book simplifying key discoveries.
- A behind-the-scenes look at what it's like working in a lab.
- A children's nonfiction book exploring cool science experiments.

Social Worker

- A collection of powerful and compassionate stories from the front lines.

- A burnout prevention and self-care guide for helpers and healers.
- A resource for families navigating the child welfare or foster system.

Somnologist (Sleep Specialist)

- A book on common sleep disorders and insomnia.
- A journal to record your dreams.
- A children's book on what happens to your body when you sleep.

Speech Therapist

- A guide for parents supporting kids with speech and language delays.
- A book of engaging speech development games and exercises.
- A children's book featuring a character going to speech therapy.

Tattoo Artist

- A visual collection of tattoo art with the stories behind each design.
- A how-to guide for aspiring artists on technique and business.
- A memoir-style book on the emotional journeys behind client tattoos.

Teacher

- A guide for new teachers navigating the first few years in the classroom.
- A memoir about the challenges and joy of teaching over time.
- A book of lesson plan ideas for a favorite subject for other teachers/homeschoolers.

Therapist (Mental Health)

- A book on emotional wellness with exercises and journal prompts.
- A myth-busting guide on therapy and mental health for the general public.
- A collection of anonymous stories of healing and transformation.

Translator

- A book on the nuances of language, culture, and meaning.
- A behind-the-scenes look at translating books, film, or live events.
- A children's story exploring words that don't exist in English.

Travel Agent

- A travel planning guide with tips for stress-free vacations.
- A book of favorite destinations, including personal stories and photos.

- A themed travel guide—e.g., "Literary Destinations for Book Lovers."

University Professor

- A niche book related to your subject area.
- A practical guide to academic publishing and tenure.
- A guide for students: how to get the most out of your college experience.

Urban Planner

- A book on the evolution of cities and the future of urban design.
- A guide to making communities more walkable, green, and inclusive.
- A visual comparison of city layouts and the stories behind them.

Urologist

- A friendly, informative guide on bladder, kidney, and men's health.
- A myth-busting book about aging and urinary health.
- A collection of patient stories and medical breakthroughs.

Veterinarian

- A pet owner's guide to preventive care and recognizing signs of an emergency.
- A memoir of heartwarming and humorous vet stories.
- A children's book about a day in the life of a vet.

Videographer

- A DIY guide to shooting high-quality video on a budget.
- A book on storytelling through video for brands and creators.

Virologist

- A science-based book explaining viruses in everyday language.
- A pandemic memoir from the lab to the front lines.
- A children's book about how our immune system fights off germs.

Virtual Assistant

- A guide to launching and scaling a VA business.
- A productivity workbook for busy entrepreneurs.
- A book of client success stories and behind-the-scenes VA tips.

Voice Coach

- A guide to vocal training for speakers, singers, or actors.

- A book on building confidence through voice and presence.
- A children's book about finding your voice—literally and figuratively.

Web Developer

- A book explaining coding for beginners, demystified.
- A guide for building and launching your first website.
- A book on freelancing and building a development business from home.

Wedding Planner

- A wedding planning guide that balances dreams and budgets.
- A book of real wedding stories with tips for avoiding pitfalls.
- A coffee table book of stunning wedding themes and designs.

Welder

- A hands-on guide to getting started with welding.
- A memoir about life in the trades and the beauty of building things.
- A photo essay book featuring creative and artistic welding projects.

Winemaker

- A book on the winemaking process from vineyard to glass.
- A memoir about reviving a family winery or starting from scratch.
- A pairing guide with recipes and stories from the cellar.

Writer

- A craft-focused book on writing techniques and inspiration.
- A personal journey through writer's block and how breakthroughs often come when you least expect them.
- A workbook of prompts and exercises for every genre.

X-ray Technician

- A behind-the-scenes guide to what happens after the "click."
- A book of strange, funny, or memorable radiology moments.
- A children's book demystifying X-rays and the hospital visit.

Xylophonist

- A guide to percussion instruments and performance techniques.

- A storybook about a xylophone that comes to life.
- A music teacher's guide to engaging kids with rhythm and melody.

Yard Designer

- An A-to-Z guide to the best plants for every garden need.
- Workbook with plant types/needs and blank yards to design your own.
- Children's book about a friendly bee.

Yoga Instructor

- A wellness book integrating breath work, poses, and mindfulness.
- A yoga journal for building a daily practice.
- A book of student transformation stories through yoga.

Youth Counselor

- A guide to supporting teens through crisis and change.
- A workbook for building confidence and emotional skills in youth.
- A collection of short stories reflecting the lives of teens today.

Zen / Meditation Coach

- A guide to mindfulness, simplicity, and present living.
- A collection of daily meditations with journaling prompts.
- A book on applying Zen principles to modern life and work.

Zookeeper

- A behind-the-scenes look at zoo life and animal care.
- A picture book about a zookeeper's busy day.
- A humorous memoir of animal escapes, antics, and heartwarming moments.

Zumba Instructor

- A book on building a dance fitness community.
- A workout journal that blends dance, fitness, and goal-setting.

BEGIN YOUR JOURNEY!

To take your journey from book idea to published success even further, visit BookologyCoach.com, where you'll find a variety of resources to support you every step of the way. Sign up for our online group, bookcamps, and coaching programs—including one-on-one coaching and exciting travel and workshop opportunities. Whether you're just getting started or ready to level up, you'll find the guidance, community, and inspiration you need to bring your book—and your business—to life.

ABOUT THE AUTHOR

Stephanie Larkin is the "head penguin" of Red Penguin Books, an independent publishing company in business for over 15 years. She enjoys working with books of all genres and helping people to "unleash their inner author" through book publishing.

At Red Penguin Books, Stephanie publishes over 100 books per year of all types and genres, ranging from business to fiction, memoir to mysteries, children's books, textbooks, and more. Red Penguin authors hail from six different continents around the world, along with most of the United States.

Stephanie is the host of *The Author Corner*—a chance to meet authors you'll want to read—airing on Verizon, Optimum, and QPTV, as well as podcast platforms everywhere.

Back on the home front, Stephanie has been married for 25+ years to her best friend Kieran—a fellow author and teacher. They have three children who are somehow wildly different yet an amazing combination of them both—a college student, an actor/artist, and an Air Force officer. They love to travel the world, and when not seeing sites from Machu Picchu to the Parthenon, they enjoy their cats and dog at home.

Stephanie's goal and company motto is *Changing lives ... one book at a time!*

ALSO BY STEPHANIE LARKIN

Launch Pad: The Countdown to Publishing Your Book

Write That Book!

Write YOUR Book!

365 Reasons to Celebrate!

SCORE with Social Media

www.ingramcontent.com/pod-product-compliance
Lightning Source LLC
Chambersburg PA
CBHW060553080526
44585CB00013B/552